IMPERIAL GERMANY

AMS PRESS
NEW YORK

Bülow

ERWIN
RAUPP
1912.

Imperial Germany

BY

PRINCE BERNHARD von BÜLOW

TRANSLATED BY

MARIE A. LEWENZ, M.A.

WITH FRONTISPIECE

NEW YORK

Dodd, Mead and Company

1914

Reprinted from the edition of 1914, New York
First AMS EDITION published 1971
Manufactured in the United States of America

International Standard Book Number: 0-404-01228-0

Library of Congress Catalog Number: 75-175039

AMS PRESS INC.
NEW YORK, N.Y. 10003

CONTENTS

FOREIGN POLICY

IMPERIAL GERMANY

FOREIGN POLICY

"In spite of the length of their history, the German people is the youngest of the great nations of Western Europe.
A period of youth has twice fallen to their lot, and with it
the struggle to establish their power as a State, and to gain
freedom for civilisation. A thousand years ago they
founded the proudest empire of the Germans; eight hundred years later they had to build up their State anew on
quite different foundations, and it is only in our times that,
as a united people, they entered the ranks of the nations."

THESE words, with which Treitschke begins his
"German History," not only show deep historical
knowledge, but also have a very modern political significance. Germany is the youngest of the Great
Powers of Europe, the *homo novus* who, having
sprung up very recently, has forced his way by his
superior capacity into the circle of the older nations.
The new Great Power was formidable after three
glorious and successful campaigns, and was looked
upon as an uninvited and unwelcome intruder, when
it entered the company of the Great Powers of Europe and demanded its share of the treasures of the

world. For centuries Europe had not believed in the possibility of the national unification of the individual German territories as one State. At any rate the European Powers had done their best to prevent this. In particular the policy of France, from the time of Richelieu to that of Napoleon III., was directed towards maintaining and intensifying the disruption of Germany, as it was rightly recognised that the ascendancy of France, *la prépondérance légitime de la France,* depended primarily on this state of affairs. Nor did the other Powers desire the unification of Germany. On this point the Emperor Nicholas and Lord Palmerston, as well as Metternich and Thiers, were at one. Nothing could show more clearly the marvellous way in which the mature wisdom of our old Emperor co-operated with the genius of Prince Bismarck than the fact that they effected the unification of Germany, not only in the face of all the difficulties with which they were confronted at home—long cherished rivalries and hatreds, all the sins of our past, and all the peculiarities of our political character, but also in spite of all opposition, avowed or secret, and of the displeasure of the whole of Europe.

Suddenly the German Empire was in existence.

More quickly even than had been feared, far stronger than anyone had guessed. None of the other Great Powers had desired the regeneration of Germany; each of them, when it actually took place, would have liked to prevent it. Small wonder that the new Great Power was not made welcome, but was looked upon as a nuisance. Even a very reserved and pacific policy could effect but little change in this first verdict. This union of the States of the Mid-European continent, so long prevented, so often feared, and at last accomplished by the force of German arms and incomparable statesmanship, seemed to imply something of the nature of a threat, or at any rate to be a disturbing factor.

In the middle of the 'nineties, in Rome, where I was Ambassador at that time, my English colleague, Sir Clare Ford, said to me: "How much pleasanter and easier it was in the world of politics when England, France and Russia constituted the tribunal of Europe, and at most Austria had to be occasionally consulted." Those good old days are past. More than forty years ago the council of Europe had to admit another member entitled to vote, one that had not only the wish to express its opinion, but also the power to act.

POLITICAL REGENERATION OF GERMANY.

A strenuous task in the history of the world had reached perfection in the masterpiece of Prince Bismarck. The unflinching purpose of the Hohenzollern dynasty for centuries required the patient heroism of the Prussian army and the resolute devotion of the Prussian people, until, after many changes of fortune, the Mark of Brandenburg rose to the rank of a Great Power, as the kingdom of Prussia. Twice the prize seemed to slip from the grasp of the Prussian State. The crushing defeat of 1806 hurled Prussia down from the dizzy heights, which had filled her contemporaries with admiration and fear, and which she had attained under the rule of the great Frederick. Those people seemed to be right who had always considered the glorious State of the great King to be nothing more than an artificial political structure, that would stand and fall with the unique political and military genius of its monarch. Its rise, after the overwhelming disasters of Jena and Tilsit, proved to an astonished world what innate and indestructible strength this State possessed. Such self-sacrifice and such heroism on the part of a whole people presuppose long-established national self-confidence. And as the people of Prussia did not rise in lawless rebellion like the much-admired Spaniards and the honest Tyrolese peasants, but placed themselves one and all, unquestioningly, at the orders of the King and his advisers, it appeared, to everyone's surprise, that amongst the Prussians consciousness as a nation and as a State were one and the same thing; and that the people had been transformed into a nation under the strict discipline of Frederick's rule. The reorganisation of the State under the guidance of men of creative power during the years 1807 to 1813 won for the Government not only the obedience of its subjects but also their affection.

In the war of liberation from 1813 to 1815 Prussia gained the respect of all, and the confidence of many of the non-Prussian Germans. The great period of upheaval and liberation endowed them with a rich inheritance. But owing to the reaction of a feeble and inglorious foreign policy, and to a home administration which never knew when to be open-handed and when to refuse, this inheritance was to a large extent squandered in the course of the following decades. Towards the end of the 'fifties in the nineteenth century, both as regards the dignity of her attitude at home and her prestige abroad, Prussia was

vastly inferior to Prussia as she had emerged from
the Wars of Liberation. True, the national movement in favour of unity had been placed on a solid
foundation by the Prussian tariff policy, but the
conference of Olmütz shattered the hopes of the German patriots who looked to Prussia for the fulfilment
of their wishes as a nation. Prussia seemed to renounce her mission of worldwide importance, and to
relinquish the policy, worthy of a Great Power, of
carrying on the work of unification—work that she
had begun with a definite politico-economical object.
Many new forces had certainly been put at the disposal of national life by the reorganisation of the
State on constitutional lines. This State would
have gained immensely, both in internal vitality and
in national striking power, if at the right time this
loyal people had been summoned to take part in
politics, as Stein and Hardenberg, Blücher and
Gneisenau, Wilhelm von Humboldt and Boyen, and
also Yorck and Bülow-Dennewitz had wished.
When the great step was taken, thirty-three years too
late, the want of confidence between the people and
the authorities was too deeply rooted, the credit of
the government had been too much damaged in the
course of the revolutionary rising, for the modern

form of government to bring about an immediate improvement. The course of Prussian policy was hampered at home by representatives of the people who were suspicious and hedged in by various doctrines, while it was checked abroad by the hitherto invincible opposition of Austria with her claims to ascendancy. Then, summoned at the critical moment by King William, almost at the eleventh hour, Bismarck took the tiller of the drifting Prussian ship of state.

The clear-sighted patriots of those times were well aware of the fact that in the normal course of historical development the union of German States under Prussian leadership must come to pass, and that it was the noblest aim of Prussian statesmanship to hasten and to bring about its consummation. But every road by which an attempt had been made to reach this end had proved impassable. As time passed, less and less seemed to be expected from the initiative of the Prussian Government. All the well-meant but unpractical efforts to induce the German people to determine its fate itself failed because of the absence of impetus from the various Governments —an impetus which is more decisive in Germany probably than in any other country. In "Wilhelm

Meister," when the melancholy Aurelia finds fault in many ways with the Germans, Lothario, a man of experience, replies that there is no better nation than the Germans, so long as they are rightly guided. The German, of whatever stock he be, has always accomplished his greatest works under strong, steady and firm guidance, and has seldom done well without such guidance, or in opposition to the Government and rulers. Bismarck himself has told us in his "Gedanken und Erinnerungen" ("Thoughts and Recollections") that he was from the first quite clear on this point. With the intuition of genius he found the way in which the hopes of the people and the interests of the German Governments might be reconciled. Probably no other statesman ever had so deep a knowledge of the history of the nation he was called upon to guide. He sought and found the motive forces of national life in the chain of events abroad. He, who was born in the year of Waterloo, and was confirmed by Schleiermacher in the Church of the Trinity in Berlin, never forgot the great times of the liberation and the rise of Prussia; at the beginning of his career as a moulder of the destinies of the world, the remembrance of these days was always with him. He realised that in Germany the will-power of the nation would not be strengthened, nor national passions roused by friction between the Government and the people, but by the clash of German pride and sense of honour with the resistance and the demands of foreign nations. So long as the question of German unification was a problem of home politics, a problem over which the political parties, and the Government and the people wrangled, it could not give birth to a mighty, compelling national movement that would sweep nations and princes alike along on a tide of enthusiasm. By making it clear that the German question was essentially a question of European politics, and when, soon after, the opponents of German unification began to move, Bismarck gave the princes the opportunity of putting themselves at the head of the national movement.

Bismarck had had a glimpse in Frankfurt, St. Petersburg, and Paris, of the cards which the Powers of Europe held. He had perceived that the unification of Germany would continue to be a purely national question only so long as it remained a vain wish, a fruitless hope of the Germans; and that it would become an international question the very moment it entered on the stage of realisation. A struggle with the opposition in Europe lay in the path of the solution of the great problem of German policy. The opposition in Germany itself could hardly be overcome except by such a struggle. By this means national policy was interwoven with international policy; with incomparable audacity and constructive statesmanship, in consummating the work of uniting Germany, he left out of play the political capabilities of the Germans, in which they have never excelled, while he called into action their fighting powers, which have always been their strongest point. By a happy dispensation of Providence Bismarck found a general such as Moltke and a military organiser such as Roon to support him. The military achievements which had enabled us to regain our position as a Great Power in Europe also assured that position. They discouraged any attempt of the Great Powers to deprive us of our right to a voice in the councils of Europe, a right which we had won in three victorious campaigns, and which has since then never been seriously disputed, although it was unwillingly granted. With the single exception of France, every one, in all probability, would have gradually become reconciled to Germany's political power if her development had ceased with the founding of the Empire. But the union of the different

States was not the end of the history of the movement, but the beginning of a new era. In the front rank of the Powers, Germany once more participated in full in the life of Europe. For a long time, however, the life of Europe had formed only a part of the life of all the nations of the world.

GERMANY AS A WORLD POWER.

Politics became more and more concerned with the world at large. The path of international politics lay open to Germany, too, when she had won a mighty position on a level with the older Great Powers. The question was whether we should tread that new path, or whether we should hesitate to undertake further hazardous enterprises for fear of compromising our newly-acquired power. In the Emperor William II. the nation found a clear-sighted, strong-willed guide, who led them along the new road. With him we trod the path of international politics; but not as conquerors, not amid adventures and quarrels. We advanced slowly, and our rate of progress was regulated, not by the impatience of ambition, but by the interests we had to promote and the rights we had to assert. We did not plunge into world politics, we grew, so to speak, into our task in that sphere, and we did not exchange the old European policy of Prussia and Germany for the new world policy; our strength to-day is rooted, as it has been since time immemorial, in the ancient soil of Europe.

"It is the task of our generation at one and the same time to maintain our position on the Continent, which is the basis of our international position, and to foster our interests abroad as well as to pursue a prudent, sensible and wisely restricted international policy, in such a way that the safety of the German people may not be endangered, and that the future of the nation may not be imperilled." With these words I attempted on November 14, 1906, towards the close of a detailed exposition of the international situation, to formulate the task which Germany must perform at the present time, and, as far as man can judge, will have to perform in the future: an international policy based on the solid foundation of our position as one of the Great Powers of Europe. At first voices were raised in protest when we trod the new paths of international politics, for it was considered a mistake to depart from the approved ways of Bismarck's Continental policy. The fact was overlooked that it was Bismarck himself who pointed out the new way to us by bringing our old policy to a close. His work, in fact, gave us access to the world of international politics. Only after the union of the States, after Germany had attained political vigour, it became possible to develop German home policy into international policy. It was not till the Empire had secured its position in Europe that it became feasible to foster the interests which German enterprise, German industry and commercial foresight had created in all quarters of the globe. It is certain that Bismarck did not foresee the course of this new development of Germany, nor the details of the problems of this new epoch; and it was not possible for him to do so. Amongst the rich treasures of political wisdom that Prince Bismarck bequeathed to us there are no universally applicable maxims, such as he formulated for a large number of eventualities in our national life, that we can make use of in our international problems. We seek in vain in the conclusions of his practical policy for a justification of the steps which our international problems exact from us. However, Bismarck also paved the way for these new and different times. We must never forget that without the gigantic achievements of Prince Bismarck, who with a mighty effort retrieved in the space of years what had been mismanaged and neglected for centuries, this new era would never have dawned. But though every new epoch of historical development is dependent on its predecessor, and derives its motive power in a greater or less degree from the past, it can only bring progress in its wake if it abandons old methods and aims and strives to attain others of its own. Even if, in the course of our new international policy, we depart from the European policy of the first Chancellor, yet it still remains true that the international tasks of the twentieth century are, properly speaking, the continuation of the work he completed in the field of Continental policy. In my speech on November 14, 1906, I pointed out that Bismarck's successors must not imitate but develop his policy. "If," I said at that time, "the course of events demands that we transcend the limits of Bismarck's aims, then we must do so."

Long ago already, the course of events drove German policy out from the narrow confines of Europe into a wider sphere. It was not ambitious restlessness which urged us to imitate the Great Powers that had long ago embarked on international politics. The strength of the nation, rejuvenated by the political reorganisation, as it grew, burst the bounds of its old home, and its policy was dictated by new interests and needs. In proportion as our national life has become international, the policy of the German Empire has become international.

In the year 1871 the number of inhabitants dwelling within the new German Empire was 41,058,792. They found work and a living in their own country, and, moreover, both were better and easier to get than before; this was due to the protection afforded by increased national power, the great improvement in the means of communication effected at the founding of the Empire, and the blessings of common legislation throughout Germany. In the year 1900 the number of inhabitants had risen to 56,367,178, and to-day it has reached more than 65,000,000. The Empire could no longer support in the old way this immense mass of humanity within its boundaries. Owing to this enormous increase of population the German State, and in consequence German policy, was confronted with a tremendous economic problem. This had to be solved, if foreign countries were not to profit by the superfluity of German life which the mother country was not able to support. In the year 1885 about 171,000 Germans emigrated; in 1892 the number was 116,339; in 1898 only 22,921; and since then the average has remained at this last low figure. Thus in the year 1885 Germany afforded the inhabitants, who numbered 20,000,000 less than to-day, inferior conditions of life to those which her 66,-000,000 subjects enjoy at the present time.

During the same period of time German foreign trade rose from the amount of 6,000 million marks to 19,160 million. Foreign trade and the means of support of a nation have an obvious connection with each other. Clearly not so much on account of the actual food imported as of the greater opportunities for work which the industries dependent on foreign trade afford. It was the development of industry that primarily led to the solution of the problem with which, owing to the increase of the population, the nation was confronted; and this solution was reached, moreover, without prejudice to the older spheres of industry, although these suffered to some extent at first, on account of the surprising speed with which the development took place. The enormous increase in number and extent of the industrial enterprises, which to-day employ millions of workmen and officials, could only be attained by winning a prominent place for German industry in the markets of the world. If at the present time it was dependent on the raw material supplied by the Continent for its manufactures, and on the European market for the sale of its goods, the gigantic proportions which modern trade has assumed would be out of the question, and millions of Germans who to-day earn their living directly through these industries, would be out of work and starving. According to the statistics, in the year 1911 raw material for industrial purposes was imported to the amount of 5,393 million, and manufactured goods to the amount of 5,460 million marks were exported. To this must be added an export of raw material, chiefly mining produce, to the amount of 2,205 million. The imports of foodstuffs amount to 3,077 million, and the exports to 1,096 million marks. These lifeless figures assume a living interest when we consider how important they are for the welfare of the Germans, and that the work and the very existence of millions of our fellow citizens depend on them. Foreign trade handles these colossal masses of goods. A very small proportion of them are transported along the railways and waterways of the Continent; by far the greater part are carried abroad by the vessels of German ship-owners. Industry, commerce, and the shipping trade have transformed the old industrial life of Germany into one of international industry, and this has also carried the Empire in political matters beyond the limits which Prince Bismarck set to German statecraft.

With its foreign trade of 19,000 millions, Germany is to-day the second greatest commercial power in the world; for it is second only to the United Kingdom with her 25,000 millions, and surpasses the United States with her 15,000 millions. In the year 1910, 11,800 German ships and 11,698 foreign ships entered the German ports, while 11,962 German and 11,678 foreign ships sailed from them. On an average the German shipyards built seventy new steamers and forty new sailing ships a year. With rapid strides we Germans have won a place in the front rank of the seafaring nations who carry on oversea trade.

THE NEED OF A NAVY.

The sea has become a factor of more importance in our national life than ever before in our history, even in the great days of the German Hansa. It has become a vital nerve which we must not allow to be severed if we do not wish to be transformed from a rising and youthfully vigorous people into a decaying and ageing one. But we were exposed to this danger as long as our foreign commerce and our mercantile marine lacked national protection at sea against the superior navies of other powers. The task that the armed forces of the German Empire had to fulfil had changed considerably since the protection on the Continent that our army secured us no longer sufficed to shield our home industries from interference, encroachment and attack. The army needed the support of a navy that we might enjoy the fruits of our national labour.

When in the spring of 1864 the English Ambassador in Berlin drew the attention of the Prussian President of the Council at that time to the excitement in England caused by Prussia's advance against Denmark, and let fall the remark that if Prussia did not cease operations the English Government might be forced to take arms against her, Herr von Bismarck-Schöhausen replied: "Well, what harm can you do us? At worst you can throw a few bombs at Stolpmünde or Pillau, and that is all." Bismarck was right at that time. We were then as good as unassailable to England with her mighty sea power, for we were invulnerable at sea. We possessed neither a great mercantile marine, the destruction of which could sensibly injure us, nor any oversea trade worth mentioning, the crippling of which we need fear.

To-day it is different. We are now vulnerable at sea. We have entrusted millions to the ocean, and with these millions the weal and woe of many of our countrymen. If we had not in good time provided protection for these valuable and indispensable national possessions, we should have been exposed to the danger of having one day to look on defencelessly while we were deprived of them. But then we could not have returned to the comfortable economic and political existence of a purely inland State. We should have been placed in the position of being unable to employ and support a considerable number of our millions of inhabitants at home. The result would have been an economic crisis which might easily attain the proportions of a national catastrophe.

THE BUILDING OF THE FLEET.

Ever since the end of the 'eighties in the nineteenth century the building of a fleet sufficient to defend our oversea interests had been a vital question for the German nation. It is greatly to the credit of the Emperor William II. that he recognised this, and devoted all the power of the throne and all the strength of his own personality to the attainment of this end. It only adds to his merit that he, as head of

the Empire, championed the building of the German
fleet at the very moment when the German people
had to come to a decision about their future, and when,
as far as man can tell, Germany had the last chance
of forging the sea weapons that she needed.

The fleet was to be built while we maintained our
position on the Continent, without our coming into
conflict with England, whom we could as yet not oppose at sea, but also while we preserved intact our
national honour and dignity. Parliamentary opposition, which at that time was considerable, could only
be overcome if steady pressure were brought to bear
on Parliament by public opinion. In view of the
anxious and discouraged state of feeling that obtained in Germany during the ten years following
Prince Bismarck's retirement, it was only possible
to rouse public opinion by harping on the string of
nationalism, and waking the people to consciousness.
A great oppression which weighed on the spirit of the
nation had been occasioned by the rupture between
the wearer of the Imperial crown and the mighty
man who had brought it up from the depths of Kyff-
häuser. This oppression could be lifted if the German Emperor could set before his people, who at
that time were not united either by common hopes or

demands, a new goal towards which to strive, and could indicate to them "a place in the sun" to which they had a right, and which they must try to attain. On the other hand, patriotic feeling must not be roused to such an extent as to damage irreparably our relations with England, against whom our sea power would for years still be insufficient, and at whose mercy we lay in 1897, as a competent judge remarked at the time, like so much butter before the knife. To make it possible to build a sufficient fleet was the foremost and greatest task of German policy after Bismarck's retirement; a task with which I also was immediately confronted, when on June 28, 1897, at Kiel, on board the *Hohenzollern*, I was entrusted by His Majesty, the Emperor, with the conduct of foreign affairs, on the same day and the same spot on which twelve years later I handed in my resignation.

On March 28, 1897, the Reichstag had passed the third reading of the Budget Committee's Report, which had made considerable reduction in the demands of the Government for ships to take the place of obsolete types, for equipment and for the construction of additional vessels. On November 27, after Admiral Hollman, till then Secretary of State at the Imperial Admiralty Office, had been replaced by a man of first-rate capabilities, Admiral von Tirpitz, the Government brought out a new Navy Bill which demanded the construction of seven additional ships of the line, of two large and seven small cruisers, fixed the date of completion of the new constructions for the end of the financial year 1904, and, by limiting the period of service of the ships, and determining what squadrons were to be kept on permanent active service, ensured the building in due time of the ships which were to take the place of out-of-date vessels. The Bill runs as follows: "Without prejudice to the rights of the Reichstag, and without demanding the imposition of new taxes, the allied Governments are not pursuing an aimless policy with regard to the navy; their sole object is to create within a definite time a national fleet, merely of such strength and power as to protect effectively the naval interests of the Empire." The Bill set the fleet on an entirely new footing. Up till then new ships had from time to time been demanded and to some extent granted; but the navy had lacked the solid foundation that the army possessed in its absolutely definite constitution. By the limitation of the period of service of the ships on the one hand, and the determination of the number of effective ships on the other, the navy became a definite constituent part of our national defence.

The building of the German fleet, like other great undertakings in the course of our national history, had to be carried out with an eye to foreign countries. It was only to be expected that this important strengthening of our national power would rouse uneasiness and suspicion in England.

THE TRADITIONAL POLICY OF ENGLAND.

The policy of no State in the world is so firmly bound by tradition as that of England; and it is in no small degree due to the unbroken continuity of her Foreign policy, handed down from century to century, pursuing its aims on definite lines, independent of the changes of party government, that England has won such magnificent success in international politics. The alpha and omega of English policy has always been the attainment and maintenance of English naval supremacy. To this aim all other considerations, friendships as well as enmities, have always been subordinated. It would be foolish to dismiss English policy with the hackneyed phrase " *perfide Albion.*" In reality this supposed treachery is nothing but a sound and justifiable egoism, which, together with other great qualities of the English people, other nations would do well to imitate.

During the second half of the eighteenth and the first half of the nineteenth centuries England lent her support to Prussia, aid which, moreover, was just at critical times in Prussian history, in the Seven Years' War, and in the time of Napoleon I. But the English attitude was hardly determined by spiritual sympathy with the kindred State in the north of Germany, struggling so manfully and laboriously to rise. To gain her own ends England supported the strongest opponent of the greatest European power; and when she had attained her object, coolly left in the lurch Frederick the Great in his hour of need, and Prussia at the Congress of Vienna. While the power of France was being strained to the uttermost by the Seven Years' War, England secured her possessions in North America. In the great years of 1813 to 1815 Prussia, with impetuous courage, finally shattered Napoleon's power. When in Vienna Prussia had to fight bitterly for every inch of land, England had already won her supremacy, and, after the downfall of her French opponent, could look upon it as assured for a considerable time. As the enemy of the strongest European power, we were England's friend. In consequence of the events of 1866 and 1870, Prussia with Germany became the greatest Power on the Continent, and to English ideas, gradually took the place that France had occupied under the *"Roi Soleil"* and the two Bonapartes. English policy followed its traditional trend and opposed the Continental Power which for the time being was strongest. After the downfall of the Habsburg rule in Spain, Bourbon France became England's natural opponent, from the time of the distinguished part played by Marlborough in the War of the Spanish Succession to that of the Alliance with the victor of the Battle of Rossbach, which was celebrated in London as a triumph of British arms. After decades of jealous mistrust of Russia, which, under Catherine II., had gained enormously in power, English policy was turned anew with full vigour against France, when Napoleon led the armies of the Republic to victory over all the States of the Continent. In the struggle between the First Empire and England, the latter was victorious, no doubt primarily owing to the unswerving and magnificent continuity of her policy, to the heroism of her bluejackets at Aboukir and Trafalgar, and the successes of the Iron Duke in

Spain, but also to the tenacity of the Russians and
Austrians, and to the impetuosity of our old Blücher
and his Prussians. When, after the fall of Napoleon, the military ascendancy seemed to move from
the west of Europe to the east, England made a political change of front. England was largely responsible for the result of the Crimean War, so
disastrous to the Russians, and for the ruin of
the ambitious plans of the proud Emperor Nicholas
I.; moreover, the Emperor Alexander II., too, found
the policy of the English barring his way, more
especially in the Near East, for so long the centre
of Russian ambitions and hopes. The English
alliance with Japan owed its birth to considerations
similar to those which led to the *entente cordiale*
with France, which latter is of great weight in the
international politics of the present day.

The interest that England takes in the balance of
power on the Continent is, of course, not confined to
the welfare of such Powers as feel themselves oppressed or threatened by the superior strength of another. Such humane sympathy rarely has decisive
influence on the political resolves of the Government
of a great State. The direction of English policy
depends primarily on the way in which the distribu-

tion of power in Europe reacts on English naval supremacy, and any shifting of the distribution of
power, which is not likely to entail such a reaction,
has always been more or less a matter of indifference
to the English Government. If England tradition-
ally—that is to say, in accordance with her unchang-
ing national interests—takes up a hostile or at least a
suspicious attitude with regard to the European
Power which for the time being is strongest, the cause
must be sought in the importance which England at-
tributes to a superior Continental Power with respect
to overseas politics. A Great Power of Europe that
has proved its military strength in so striking a manner that, in the normal course of affairs, it need fear
no attack on its frontiers has practically developed
the conditions of national existence by means of which
England has become the greatest sea and commercial
power in the world. England with her strength and
her courage, could fare forth unconcernedly on the
ocean, for she knew that, having the sea for a protection, her borders were safe from hostile attacks. If
the borders of a Continental Power are similarly protected by the fear which its victorious and superior
army inspires, it obtains the freedom of action in oversea affairs which England owes to her geographical

position. It becomes a competitor in the field in which England claims supremacy. In this, English policy is based on historical experience—one might almost say on the law of the evolution of nations and states. Every nation with sound instincts and a viable organisation of the State, has attempted to win its way to the sea coast if, owing to its geographical position, it had no coast-line. The bitterest and most protracted struggles have always raged round coast-lines and harbours, from Corcyra and Potidæa, which were the cause of the Peloponnesian War, to Kavalla, about which the Greeks and Bulgarians quarrelled in our times. Nations which could not reach the sea, or were forced away from it, silently retired from the universal contest. Now the possession of the coast-line means neither more nor less than the opportunity to develop oversea power, and, finally, the opportunity to transform Continental politics into international politics. Those European nations that have not made use of their coasts and harbours for this purpose, were unable to do so because they required all their forces to defend their borders against their opponents on the Continent. Thus the extensive colonial schemes of the Great Elector had to be abandoned by his successors.

Access to the paths of international politics was always easiest for the strongest Continental Power. But England guarded these paths. When Louis XIV. proposed a Franco-English alliance to Charles II., the English king, who, in other respects was very friendly to the French, replied that certain obstacles stood in the way of a sincere alliance, and that the most considerable of these were the efforts France was making to become a Sea Power that would compel respect. For England, whose only importance lay in her commerce and her fleet, this would be such a cause of suspicion that every step which France took in that direction would rouse afresh the jealousy between the two nations.

After the conclusion of the Peace of Hubertusburg, the elder Pitt expressed in Parliament his regret that France had been afforded the opportunity to build up her fleet again. It was mainly as an opponent of French oversea policy that England took sides against France in the war of the Spanish Succession, a war which dealt France's supremacy in Europe the first searching blow, and in which England not only obtained the key of the ocean by winning Gibraltar, but also gained possession of the heart of Canada, for which France had fought so strenuously. In the middle of the eighteenth century Lord Chatham said: "The only danger that England need fear will arise on the day that sees France attain the rank of a great sea, commercial, and Colonial power."   And before the Crimean War David Urquhart wrote: "Our insular position leaves us only the choice between omnipotence and impotence.   Britannia will either become mistress of the seas or will be swallowed up by them."   English policy has remained true to itself up to the present time, because England is still, as she was formerly, the first Sea Power.   Subtler diplomatic conflicts have taken the place of the more violent struggles of olden times.   The political aim remains the same.

GERMANY AND ENGLAND.

When Germany, after the solution of her Continental problems—after securing her power in Europe —was neither willing nor able to refrain from embarking on international politics, she was bound to inconvenience England.   The consequences of this turn of affairs could be mitigated by diplomacy, they could not be prevented.

But even if we can understand the traditions of English policy, such understanding in no wise im-

plies the admission that England has any reason to
contemplate with mistrust the expansion of German
national industries into international industries, of
German Continental policy into international policy,
and especially the construction of a German navy.
This mistrust was perhaps justified in other centuries in the case of other Powers.

The course of our international policy differs completely in means as well as ends, from the old-time attempts at conquering the world made by Spain,
France, and at one time by Holland and Russia.
The international policy against which England made
such a determined stand in the past mostly aimed at
a more or less violent change in the international situation. We only keep in view the change in the conditions of our national life. The international policy of other countries which England opposed was of
an offensive nature, ours is defensive. It was both
necessary and desirable for us to be so strong at sea
that no Sea Power could attack us without grave risk,
so that we might be free to protect our oversea interests, independently of the influence and the choice of
other Sea Powers. Our vigorous national development, mainly in the industrial sphere, forced us to
cross the ocean. For the sake of our interests, as

well as of our honour and dignity, we were obliged to
see that we won for our international policy the same
independence that we had secured for our European
policy. The fulfilment of this national duty might
eventually be rendered more difficult by English opposition, but no opposition in the world could release
us from it.

Our fleet had to be built with an eye to English
policy—and in this way it was built. My efforts in
the field of international politics had to be directed to
the fulfilment of this task. For two reasons Germany had to take up an internationally independent
position. We could not be guided in our decisions
and acts by a policy directed against England, nor
might we, for the sake of England's friendship, become dependent upon her. Both dangers existed,
and more than once were perilously imminent. In
our development as a Sea Power we could not reach
our goal either as England's satellite, or as her antagonist. England's unreserved and certain friendship
could only have been bought at the price of those very
international plans for the sake of which we had
sought British friendship. Had we followed this
course we should have made the mistake to which the
Roman poet refers when he says that one must not

"propter vitam vivendi perdere causas." But as England's enemy we should have had little prospect of reaching such a point in our development as a Sea and Commercial Power as we have actually attained.

GERMANY AND ENGLAND DURING THE BOER WAR.

During the Boer War, which strained the forces of the British Empire to the uttermost, and led England into great difficulties, there seemed to be an opportunity of dealing the secret opponent of our international policy a shrewd blow. As in the rest of Europe, enthusiasm for the Boers ran high in Germany. Had the Government undertaken to put a spoke in England's wheel, it would have been sure of popular approval. To many it seemed that the European situation was favourable to a momentary success against England, and that French assistance was assured. But there was only a seeming community of interests against England in Europe, and any eventual political success against England in the Boer question would have had no real value for us. An attempt to proceed to action at the bidding of the pro-Boer feelings of that time would soon have had a sobering effect. Among the French the deeply rooted national hatred against the German Empire would speedily and completely have ousted the momentary ill-feeling against England as soon as we had definitely committed ourselves to a course hostile to her interests; and a fundamental change of front in French policy would have resulted directly after. However painful the memory of the then recent events at Fashoda might be to French pride, it could not suffice to turn the scale against the memory of Sedan. The Egyptian Sudan and the White Nile had not driven the thought of Metz and Strassburg from the hearts of the French. There was great danger that we should be thrust forward against England by France, who at the psychological moment would refuse her aid. As in Schiller's beautiful poem, "Die Ideale" ("The Ideals"), our companions would have vanished midway.

But even if, by taking action in Europe, we had succeeded in thwarting England's South African policy, our immediate national interests would not have benefited thereby. From that moment onward for many a long day our relations with England would have been poisoned. England's passive resistance to the international policy of *new* Germany would have changed to very active hostility. During those years we were occupied in founding our sea power by building the German navy, and even in the event of defeat in the South African War, it was possible for England to stifle our sea power in the embryo. Our neutral attitude during the Boer War had its origin in weighty considerations of the national interests of the German Empire.

Our navy was not strong enough for us forcibly to achieve a sufficient sea power in the teeth of English interests. Nor could we, by being towed in the wake of English policy, reach the desired goal of possessing a strong fleet.

DISCUSSION IN THE PRESS ABOUT THE POSSIBILITY OF AN ANGLO-GERMAN ALLIANCE.

The thought occurred to many that English opposition against German international policy, and above all against the construction of a German navy, might be overcome most easily by an alliance between Germany and England. Indeed, at times the idea of an Anglo-German alliance has been discussed in the Press of both countries. It had already occupied Bismarck's thoughts, but the final result was only the resigned remark: "We would be willing enough to love the English, but they will not allow us to do so." Later on, too, Germany might perhaps not have been disinclined to conclude a treaty with England, on a basis of absolute equality and with mutual obligations. German interests would have gained nothing by stipulations which England might disregard in the event of a change of Ministry, or the occurrence of any other circumstances over which we had no control, while we continued bound to them. Nor would it have sufficed us that some Minister or other was in favour of an Anglo-German treaty. To make a lasting agreement the whole Cabinet, and above all the Prime Minister, would have had to support it. Bismarck pointed out how difficult it was to establish firm relations with England, because treaties of long duration were not in accordance with English traditions, and the expression of opinion of English politicians, even those in a prominent position, and the transitory moods of the English Press were by no means equivalent to immutable pledges. For many reasons English public opinion is more favourable to France than to us, for England no longer looks upon her as a rival, and certainly not as a serious competitor, at sea; consequently France occupies a different position from ours with regard to England. In consideration of the widespread jealousy roused in England by Germany's industrial progress, and especially by the increase of the German navy, it was only on condition of absolutely binding pledges on the part of England that we could have set foot on the bridge of an Anglo-German alliance. We could only thus unite ourselves with England on the assumption that the bridge which was to help us over the real and supposed differences between England and Germany was strong enough to bear our weight.

At the time this question of an alliance was being ventilated the European situation differed in many respects from the present one. Russia had not then been weakened by the Japanese War, but intended to secure and expand her newly-won position in the Far East, in particular on the Gulf of Pechili. Owing to the Asiatic questions pending between the two empires, relations between England and Russia were then rather strained. The danger was imminent that if Germany allied herself with England she would have to undertake the rôle against Russia that Japan assumed later single-handed. But we should have had to play this part under very different conditions from the very favourable ones which Japan found at her disposal in her conflict with Russia. The Japanese War was unpopular in Russia, and it had to be waged at an immense distance, like a colonial war. If we had allowed ourselves to be thrust forward against Russia we should have found ourselves in a far more difficult position. A war against Germany would not, in these circumstances, have been unpopular in Russia, and would on the part of the Russians have been carried on with that national enthusiasm which is peculiar to them when defending their native soil. France would have preferred the excuse of the *casus foederis,* and would have been able to wage her war of revenge under favourable circumstances. England was on the eve of the Boer War. Her position would have been improved if her great colonial enterprise had been supported and accompanied by a European complication, such as had rendered her good service in the middle of the eighteenth and in the first decade of the nineteenth centuries. In the event of a general conflict, we Germans would have had to wage strenuous war on land in two directions, while to England would have fallen the easier task of further extending her Colonial Empire without much trouble, and of profiting by the general weakening of the Continental Powers. Last, but certainly not least, while military operations were going forward on the Continent, and for a long time after, we should have found neither strength nor means nor leisure to proceed with the building of our navy, as we have been able to do. Thus the only course left to us was not to entrench upon English interests and to avoid both a hostile encounter and docile dependence.

ENGLAND AND THE GERMAN NAVY.

Thus, unaffected and uninfluenced by England, we have succeeded in creating that power at sea which is the real basis of our industrial interests and our international policy; a power that the strongest enemy would not attack without hesitation.

During the first ten years after the introduction of the Navy Bill of 1897, and while our shipbuilding was in its infancy, an English Government, ready to go to any lengths, could have made short work of our development as a Sea Power, and rendered us harmless before we grew formidable at sea. Such action against Germany was repeatedly demanded in England. The Civil Lord of the Admiralty, Mr. Arthur Lee, asserted in a public speech on February 3, 1905, that attention should be directed to the North Sea, the British fleet should concentrate there, and in the event of war they must "strike the first blow, before

the other side found time to read in the newspapers
that war had been declared." The *Daily Chronicle*
emphasised this utterance with the words: "If the
German fleet had been smashed in October, 1904,
we should have had peace in Europe for sixty years.
For this reason we consider the statement Mr. Arthur
Lee uttered, assuming that it was on behalf of the
Cabinet, a wise and pacific declaration of the unalter-
able purpose of the Mistress of the Seas."   In the autumn of 1904 the *Army and Navy Gazette* remarked
how intolerable it was that England alone, owing to
the existence of the German fleet, was forced to adopt
measures of defence which she would otherwise not
have needed. The article runs: "Once before we
had to snuff out a fleet, which we believed might be
employed against us. There are many people, both
in England and on the Continent, who consider the
German fleet the only serious menace to the preservation of peace in Europe. Be that as it may, we
are content to point out that the present moment is
particularly favourable to our demand that the German fleet shall not be further increased." About the
same time an English review of good standing wrote:
"If the German fleet were destroyed the peace of
Europe would be assured for two generations. Eng-

land and France, or England and the United States,
or all three, would guarantee the freedom of the sea
and prevent the building of more ships, which, in
the hands of ambitious Powers, with a growing
population and no Colonies, are dangerous weapons."

Just at this time France was preparing to injure
us in Morocco. A few months earlier, in June, 1904,
a French publicist told me that the construction of
our fleet called forth widespread and increasing anxiety in England; that England could not make up
her mind how best to put a stop to our further shipbuilding, whether by direct representations or by en-
couraging the Chauvinistic elements in France. To-
day England gives us our due as a Sea Power—as
the strongest Sea Power next to themselves. When,
in the winter of 1909, an English Member of Parliament stated the fact that England would not have
needed to continue her sea armaments at such a fever-
ish rate if she had ten years previously prevented the
rise of the German Sea Power, he expressed a thought
that, so far as the policy of mere force is concerned,
is comprehensible and perhaps to the point. But
England would not have found an opportunity to
nip our growing fleet in the bud, a thing she had re-

peatedly done in the past in the case of other countries, because we did not expose ourselves.

THE PEACEFUL AIMS OF GERMAN WORLD POLICY.

The fleet that we have built since 1897, and that,
though far inferior to England's, has made us the
second Sea Power of the world, enables us to support
our interests everywhere with all the weight of our
reputation as a Great Power. The foremost duty
of our navy is to protect our world commerce and the
lives and honour of our fellow-countrymen abroad.
German battleships have performed this task in the
West Indies and the Far East. Emphatically, it is
a largely defensive rôle that we assign to our fleet.
It is self-understood that this defensive rôle might
become an offensive one in serious international conflicts. If the Empire should be wantonly attacked,
from no matter what quarter, the sea, as a theatre of
war, will have a very different and much greater importance in our times than it did in 1870. In such a
case the fleet as well as the army would, needless to
say, in accordance with Prussian and German traditions, consider attack the best form of defence. But
there is absolutely no ground for the fear which the
building of our navy has aroused, that with the rise of

German power at sea the German love of battle will be awakened.

Of all the nations of the world the Germans are the people that have most rarely set out to attack and conquer. If we except the expeditions against Rome, led by the German Emperors in the Middle Ages, which originated rather in a grand if mistaken political illusion than in love of battle and conquest, we shall seek in vain in our past for wars of conquest that may be compared with those of France in the seventeenth, eighteenth and nineteenth centuries, those of Spain under the Habsburgs, of Sweden in her best days, or those of the Russian and British Empires in the course of their fundamentally expansive national policy. For centuries we Germans have aimed at nothing but the defence and security of our country. Just as the Great King did not lead his unvanquished battalions on adventurous expeditions, after the conquest of Silesia and the safeguarding of the independence of the Prussian monarchy, so the Emperor William and Bismarck, after the unparalleled successes of two great wars, did not dream of attempting further military exploits. If any nation may boast of political self-restraint, it is the Germans. We have always set a limit to our successes ourselves, and have not waited till the exhaustion of our national resources made us halt. Consequently our evolution lacks periods of a brilliant and sudden rise; rather it is a slow and unwearied advance. The Germans have practically no tinge of that restlessness which in other nations urges men to find in success the spur to further bold effort. Our political character is less that of the rash, speculative merchant than that of the plodding peasant who, after sowing carefully, patiently awaits the harvest.

After the Franco-German War all the world was filled with dread of further military enterprises on the part of Germany. There was no scheme of conquest, however improbable, that we were not credited with harbouring. Since then more than four decades have passed. The strength of our people has grown, we are richer in material possessions, and our army has become stronger and stronger. The German fleet has been created and developed. The number of great wars that have been waged since 1870 exceeds the average for such a period of time in earlier years. Germany did not seek to take part in any of them, and calmly resisted all attempts to be drawn into military entanglements.

Without boastfulness or exaggeration, we may say

that never in the course of history has any **Power,** possessing such superior military strength as the Germans, served the cause of peace in an equal measure. This fact cannot be explained by our well-known and undoubted love of peace. The German has always been peace-loving, and has nevertheless had to draw his sword again and again in order to defend himself against foreign attacks. As a matter of fact, peace has primarily been preserved, not because Germany herself did not attack other nations, but because other nations feared a repulse in the event of their attacking Germany. The strength of our armaments has proved to be a more effective guarantee of peace than any in the last tumultuous centuries. An historical judgment is contained in this fact.

Given a rightly guided foreign policy, the completion of our Lines of Defence by the navy constitutes an additional and increased guarantee of peace. Just as the army prevents any wanton interruption of the course of Germany's Continental policy, so the navy prevents any interruption in the development of our world policy. As long as we had no navy, our rapidly growing international industrial interests, which are also inalienably bound up with our national economic interests, presented a vulnerable surface to our opponents. By protecting this weak point, and also rendering a naval attack on the Empire an undertaking of great risk for the enemy, we preserved not only the peace of our own country, but also that of Europe. We were concerned with the acquirement of means of defence, not of attack. After entering the ranks of the Sea Powers we continued quietly on the same course as heretofore. The new era of unbounded German world-policy, which was so often foretold abroad, has not dawned. But we certainly have acquired the means of effectively protecting our interests, of resisting aggression, and of maintaining and developing our position everywhere, especially in Asia Minor and Africa.

As our problems in world-politics increased, the web of our international relations had to be extended. Distant oversea States, which at the time of our purely Continental policy concerned us but little, grew of more and more importance to us. It became the most significant duty of our present-day policy to cultivate good and, if possible, friendly relations with these. This refers primarily to the two Great Powers of the West and the East, the United States of America

and Japan. In both cases we had to overcome temporary differences before there could be any question of entering into friendly relations.

GERMANY AND THE UNITED STATES.

During the Spanish-American War a section of
German public opinion manifested strong sympathy
with Spain, which was resented in the States. German relations with America had also been clouded by
the way in which part of the English and American
Press had interpreted certain incidents which had occurred between our squadrons and the American fleet
off Manila. This difference reached its height in
February, 1899, so that it seemed desirable strongly
to advocate preparations for a better understanding
between the two nations of kindred race. What I
said on this point in the Reichstag has subsequently
proved true. "From the point of view of a common-
sense policy, there is no reason why the best relations
should not subsist between Germany and America.
I see no single point in which the German and American interests are opposed, nor any in the future where,
in the course of their development, they are likely to
clash. We can say without hesitation that during the
last century the United States have nowhere found

better understanding or juster recognition than in
this country." More than anyone else the Emperor
William II. manifested this understanding and appreciation of the United States of America. It was
he who first paved the way for our friendly and sound
relations. He won over the Americans by his consistently friendly and sympathetic attitude. He was
bound to President Roosevelt by ties of personal
friendship. The mission of Prince Henry to America was crowned with the success we had anticipated.
It contributed largely to making both nations realise
how many common interests united them, and how
few real differences divided them. It was a happy
thought of the Emperor's, too, to knit the two Germanic nations together intellectually, by the exchange
of teachers of repute in the German and American
Universities. German intellect, poetry, philosophy,
and science have met nowhere with more sincere admiration than in the United States. On the other hand
Germany, more than any other country, studied and
welcomed the wonderful technical inventions of
America. This intimate exchange of ideas in the
field of intellectual and scientific achievement found
its outward manifestation in the arrangements for
exchanging professors. These ties between the two

nations and also between their rulers, as they grew
closer, prompted a friendly political relation between
us and the United States.   Not only did we settle
the question of Samoa amicably, but during the critical period through which our country passed at the
beginning of the new century America never once
opposed our policy.   With the exception of Austria,
there is probably no country where existing circumstances contribute so naturally to permanent friendly
relations with us as in North America.   About 12,-
000,000 Germans live in the United States.   Since
the formation of the "Deutsch-Amerikanischen Na-
tionalbund" (National German-American Union)
in 1910, they are animated more and more by the desire to maintain and encourage a close connection
with their old German home, while at the same time
remaining perfectly loyal to their adopted country.
As long as policy in Germany and in America is directed by cool-headed men, who avoid with equal
scrupulousness exaggerated expressions of friendship or nervous impatience when confronted with occasional differences (which can always arise in the
sphere of industry), we need not fear for our relations
with the United States.   Respect for each other, on
the basis and within the bounds of self-respect, will

be the best means of preserving our friendship with America.

GERMANY AND JAPAN.

Our relations with Japan, as with the United States of America, passed through a period of strain towards the end of the nineteenth century. Up to the bginning of the 'nineties we had served as a model for the Japanese and had been their friend. This warlike nation of the Far East warmly admired our military organisation and our warlike history; and after the defeat of China the Japanese boasted that they were the Prussians of the East. Our relations with them received a severe shock when, in 1895, we together with France and Russia forced victorious Japan to reduce her demands on China. When we thus interfered with Japan we lost much of the sympathy which she had for many years accorded us, and we did not earn particular gratitude from France and Russia. The German Emperor's scheme, which was to have served the ideal of promoting peace, was eagerly and successfully taken advantage of by our antagonists and competitors to injure us with the Japanese. By dint of prolonged efforts we succeeded at last in reviving a better state of feeling towards Germany in Japan.

It is not to our interest to have that eminently capable and brave nation for an enemy. On the other hand, we have no intention, of course, of allowing Japan to use us as a catspaw. It would have very considerably facilitated matters not only for Japan but also for England if, for the sake of their interests in the Far East, we had allowed ourselves to be thrust forward against Russia. We ourselves should have fared badly in the matter. Just as we did not welcome the idea of offending and estranging Japan for the sake of France and Russia, so we did not care to fall out with Russia on account of the interests in the Far East of other Powers.

Towards the end of the 'eighties Prince Bismarck once said to me, with reference to Russia and Asia: "In Russia there is a very serious amount of unrest and agitation, which may easily result in an explosion. It would be best for the peace of the world if the explosion took place in Asia and not in Europe. We must be careful not to stand just in the way, otherwise we may have to bear the brunt of it." If we had allowed ourselves to be thrust forward against Russia before the Russo-Japanese War, we should have had to bear the brunt. I also heard him say on some occasion: "If Mr. N. proposes something to you that would be useful to him and harmful to you, it does not by any means follow that Mr. N. is a fool. But you are a fool if you agree to it."

CONTINENTAL POLICY AND WORLD POLICY.

If Germany, after attaining the great aim of her Continental policy, is in a position, with her largely increased and steadily increasing powers, to reach out into the wide world, that by no means implies that we are at liberty to expend the whole of our national strength on enterprises outside the Continent of Europe.

The transition to international politics has opened to us new political courses and discovered to us new national problems; but it does not imply the abandonment of all our old courses, or a fundamental change in our tasks. Our new world-policy is an extension, not a shifting of the field of our political activities.

We must never forget that the consolidation of our position as a Great Power in Europe has made it possible for us to transform our industrial activity from a national into an international one, and our Continental policy into international policy. Our world-policy is based upon the successes of our European

policy. The moment the firm foundation constituted by Germany's position as a Great European
Power begins to totter, the whole fabric of our world-
policy will collapse. It is quite possible that a defeat in international politics might leave our position
in Europe unchanged; but it is unthinkable that a
sensible diminution of power and influence in Europe
would leave our position in international politics un-
shaken. We can only pursue our world-policy on
the basis of our European policy. The conservation
of our position of power on the Continent is still, as
it was in Bismarck's day, the first and last aim of
our national policy. If, at the behest of our national
needs, we have gone beyond Bismarck in international
affairs, nevertheless we must always maintain the
principles of his European policy as the firm ground
on which we take our stand. The new era must be
rooted in the traditions of the old. A healthy development may in this case, too, be ensured by a common-sense compromise between the old and the new,
between preservation and progress. To renounce
international politics would have been equivalent to
condemning our national vitality to slow but sure
decay. An adventurous international policy, which

should take no account of our old European interests, might at first seem attractive and impressive, but it would soon lead to a crisis if not to a catastrophe in our development.

Sound political success is achieved much in the same way as mercantile success; by keeping a steady course between the Scylla of over-carefulness and the Charybdis of speculation. A conflict between Germany and England would be a great misfortune for both countries, for Europe and for mankind in general. Ever since the day when I undertook the affairs of the Foreign Office, I have been convinced that such a conflict would never come to pass:—

i. If we built a fleet which could not be attacked without very grave risk to the attacking party.

ii. If we did not, beyond that, indulge in undue and unlimited shipbuilding and armaments, and did not overheat our marine boiler.

iii. If we allowed no Power to injure our reputation or our dignity.

iv. If we allowed nothing to make an irremediable breach between us and England. That is why I always repelled any impertinent attack which was likely to hurt our feelings as a nation, from whatever quarter it came, but resisted all temptations to interfere in the Boer War, as that would have dealt English self-esteem a wound that would not heal.

v. If we kept calm and cool, and neither injured England nor ran after her.

"The basis of a sound and sensible world-policy is a strong, national home policy." So I said in December, 1901, when a member of the Reichstag, Eugen Richter, tried to prove that the policy, which underlay the new tariff and aimed at the protection of home industries and especially agrarian interests, was antagonistic to the new world-policy which was founded on the interests of commerce. The apparent antagonism between the two was really a compromise; for German industrial activity in the international field had had its origin in the extremely flourishing condition of home industries.

The connection between politics and national industry is far closer in our times than it was in the past. The home and foreign policies of modern States re-act directly upon the fluctuations and changes of their very highly developed industrial life, and every considerable industrial interest ultimately finds political expression in one way or another. International commerce, with all the various interests depending on it, has made our international policy a necessity. Our industrial activities at home demand a corresponding home policy. Between the two, some compromise must be sought and found.

Seven years after the tariff debates the worth of this compromise between the home policy and international policy, much discussed then in political and industrial circles, was proved in the sphere of international politics on the occasion of the Bosnian crisis in the year 1908. This event demonstrates more clearly than any academic discussion could do the real relation in which our oversea policy and our European policy stand to one another. German policy, up to the time when the Bosnian question was raised, was mainly controlled by consideration of our international policy. Not that Germany directed her foreign relations in accordance with her oversea interests, but that England's displeasure at the development of German foreign trade and especially at the growth of German sea power, influenced the grouping of the Powers and their attitude towards the German Empire. Public opinion amongst the English, who are usually so cool and courageous, gave way temporarily to fear of a German invasion; and this fear was so groundless and so senseless that it almost amounted to a panic. This, moreover, was systematically encouraged by a large section of the English Press, which has a very powerful and widespread influence.

THE ENGLISH POLICY OF ISOLATION.

Since the beginning of the new century the influence of King Edward VII. had made itself felt in English foreign politics. He was a monarch of extraordinary insight into the character of men, who knew to a nicety the art of handling them, and had wide and varied experience. English policy did not so much aim at directly opposing the interests of Germany as at gradually checkmating her by shifting the Balance of Power in Europe. By a series of *ententes,* for the sake of which considerable British interests were several times sacrificed, she sought to attach to herself the other states of Europe, and so to isolate Germany. It was the period of the so-called English policy of isolation. With Spain she concluded a treaty with reference to the Mediterranean. France, of course, was well disposed towards the opponent of the German Empire, and the Franco-British treaty about Egypt and Morocco in the year 1904 drove the memory of Fashoda into the background.

Russia also drew near to England, for owing to the after-effects of the heavy losses by land and at sea that she had sustained in her war with Japan, and also because of serious disturbances at home, she had decided to come to an arrangement with England about their respective spheres of interest in Asia. Italy was eagerly wooed. Similar attempts with regard to Austro-Hungary, on the occasion of the meeting of the monarchs at Ischl, failed, thanks to the unswerving loyalty to his ally of the old Emperor, Franz Joseph.

In Algeciras, although Germany defended her own national interests as part and parcel of the general, international interests, we had a hard fight against the French demands which had England's support.

At that time the policy of isolation to all appearances succeeded with regard to the grouping of the Powers; and yet the aims of German policy in respect of Morocco were practically fulfilled by the very fact that the conference was called, and by the more important decisions it made. The question was, how the system of *ententes* would work in the sphere of purely European politics.

THE BOSNIAN CRISIS.

The final annexation by Austro-Hungary of the Provinces of Bosnia and Herzegovina which, in accordance with the decisions of the Berlin Congress, Austria had occupied since 1878, led to a great European crisis. Russia opposed these proceedings on the part of Austria. Believing that an armed settlement of the old Austro-Russian rivalry in the Balkans was at hand, Servia, whose plans for aggrandisement would be thwarted, thought herself entitled to take up arms against the Danube Monarchy. England sided with Russia, and the language of the English Press was almost more impassioned than the utterances of the Russians. The antagonistic policy of England seemed aimed less against Austria than against Germany, Austria's ally. For the first time the Austro-German alliance was to prove its durability and strength in a grievous conflict.

In my speeches in the Reichstag I made it quite clear that Germany was resolved to preserve her alliance with Austria at any cost. The German sword had been thrown into the scale of European decision, directly in support of our Austro-Hungarian ally, indirectly for the preservation of European peace, and above all for the sake of German credit and the maintenance of our position in the world. It would now be made manifest whether Germany really had been checkmated by the policy of isolation, and whether the Powers that had been drawn into the circle of Anti-German policy would find it consistent with their vital interests in Europe to take up a hostile attitude towards the German Empire and its allies. The course of the Bosnian crisis, in point of fact, made an end of the policy of isolation. No power was willing to subordinate its own European interests to the international interests of foreigners, or to sacrifice itself for others. The group of Powers whose influence had been so much overestimated at Algeciras, fell to pieces when faced with the tough problems of Continental policy. Italy sided with her allies, France awaited events and assumed an attitude not unfriendly to Germany, and the Emperor Nicholas gave the world a new proof of his wisdom and his love of peace by deciding on a friendly settlement of the existing difficulties. The ingenious isolation of Germany, for some time the terror of timid souls, proved to be a diplomatic illusion devoid of political actuality. The fundamental error in the calculations had been this, that they had not set down at its full value as a factor in the situation the importance of the German Empire as a Great Power of Europe. It was certain that if anyone succeeded in dealing our position in Europe a keen blow, our international policy would sustain a mortal wound. In that, which was one of the premises on which the policy of isolation was based, calculations were correct. But we are not so easy to wound in our Continental position. The Triple Alliance is a force against which no country would let itself be thrust forward for the sake of remote interests, even if very clever diplomacy were employed in the attempt. It is a force with which no Power would dare to wage war except as a last resort in a vital question. Last, but not least, the Continental Powers are bound by many ties of common interest which cannot be subordinated to the rivalry of Germany and England at sea and in commerce. With regard to international politics, England is the only country with which Germany has an account. As far as all the other European Powers are concerned, the contra-account of Continental politics is the decisive factor in the attitude they assume towards Germany.

This was the great lesson of the Bosnian crisis,

that our international policy, when all is said and done, is based on our Continental policy. The former brought us into conflict with England. The policy of isolation, which seemed likely to endanger our safety, was directed against the international trade and the sea power of Germany. By means of our strength as a Continental Power, we tore the web which encompassed us. The result was that a tide of sober reflection set in on the other side of the Channel, and this was the necessary forerunner of a period in which a calm exchange of ideas and a sensible adjustment of interests took place between the two nations.

In the winter of 1909, immediately after the Bosnian crisis had taken a decisive turn, King Edward VII. paid a visit to the German Emperor and Empress in Berlin. This visit passed off in a satisfactory manner, and the king had a hearty reception. He, for his part, succeeded in emphasising the favourable impression made by his visit, by repeatedly giving expression to his sincere love of peace and his warm friendship, sentiments which found corroboration soon after in the Speech from the Throne and the Debate on the Address in the English Parliament.

This last visit of King Edward VII. aroused good hope for the future and shed a pleasant light, not only on the personal relations of the King with Germany, but also on those between two great nations who have every reason to respect one another, and to vie with each other amicably in the work of peace. Reactions might, of course, set in. In point of fact they did. Indeed, the reaction in the summer of 1911 was somewhat violent. But the attempt to extend the opposition between England and Germany into a system of combined international policy, will hardly be repeated, and, if it should be, it will once more be foiled by the hard facts of Continental politics, of which the very hardest is the Triple Alliance.

THE TRIPLE ALLIANCE.

European history has seldom, if ever, seen an alliance of such strength and durability as the Triple Alliance. In the year 1879 Bismarck concluded the alliance with Austro-Hungary; in 1883 Italy joined it. For thirty years now the treaties of alliance have been regularly renewed, and there has never been any ground for the hopes of its ill-wishers and the fears of its well-wishers with regard to the durability of the Triple Alliance. In so far as a term of party politics can be applied to international politics, which, of course, differ completely in aim, cause, and effect, one may characterise the Triple Alliance as one with emphatically conservative tendencies. Herein, probably, the chief cause of its strength must be sought. It was neither desire of conquest nor unsatisfied ambition that brought the States of the Triple Alliance together, and keeps them united. The three mid-European States are bound to each other by the firm resolve to maintain the existing balance of power in Europe, and should a forcible change be attempted, to prevent it if need be by force. The united strength of Middle Europe stands in the path of any revolution—any European policy which might elect to follow the courses pursued by Louis XIV. or Napoleon I. This alliance is like a mighty fortification dividing the Continent in two. The wish to maintain existing conditions implies, as far as international politics is concerned, a desire for peace. The founders of the Triple Alliance intentionally created a guarantee of peace. They have not been disappointed in their hopes, for the steadfastness of the Triple Alliance has more than once in the course of the last thirty years warded off the rising danger of war.

ITALY.

The attitude of Italy towards the Triple Alliance has undergone many a change in the course of thirty years; these changes in Italy were due partly to internal political events, partly to the peculiar development of certain Mediterranean questions. But our opponents did not succeed in severing Italy's connection with the Triple Alliance, although at times they made pertinacious and eager attempts to do so.

The relations between Italy and Austria are naturally more complex than the terms on which we stand with Italy. The memory of the passionate struggle lasting for half a century, which the Italian people carried on against the Austrian dominion in Italy, has not yet faded. Such recollections are kept fresh in the mind of the nation by monuments, inscriptions, a voluminous literature, and the fiery patriotism of the Italians. Moreover, the fact that nearly a million Italians belong to the Monarchy of the Habsburgs has repeatedly, and at times injuriously, influenced Austro-Italian relations. That will always remain a sore point. Many an Italian regards his kindred in Austria with a passion that is very far removed from the calm which our great statesman recommended to us in respect of our kindred in foreign lands and especially in Austro-Hungary. Italians and Austrians should both remember the truth of the statement which a distinguished Italian statesman, the Ambassador Count Nigra, once expressed to me in the following words: "Austria and Italy can only be either allies or enemies." The interests of both countries, if rightly understood, require them to remain allies. Italy and Germany are so obviously interdependent that they are always bound to unite. This interdependence is due to many and weighty considerations; the absence of all rivalry between the nations, and—since the memory of the struggle in the Tentoburger Wald and of the Battle of Legnano has grown faint with time—the absence of any disturbing reminiscence, the similarity of their historical development, and the common dangers which might threaten them in like manner.

Our relations with Italy are, contrary to the accepted view of the character of the two nations, regarded by us from the sentimental, and by the Italians from the common-sense, point of view. We are apt at times to deprecate these relations unduly, and at times to value them too highly from an excess of sentimentality. Neither at Algeciras, nor on account of her Tripoli expedition, nor shortly before, at the interview at Racconigi, did Italy ever contemplate severing her connection with us. A host of legends has arisen around the attitude that Italy adopted at the Conference of Algeciras. It has been asserted that at Algeciras Italy left us in the lurch, or even that she played a double game with us, and this idea gave rise amongst us for a time to a totally unfounded mistrust of Italy's loyalty to the alliance. The fact is, that on a few minor questions Italy voted with the Western Powers and against us. These votes were cleverly taken up by the French Press, and were presented to the world as an indication that Italy would renounce the Triple Alliance and enter into friendly relations with France. In other and more important questions, Italy supported our point of view at Algeciras, and furthered our wishes. Our representative at Algeciras, Herr von Radowitz, always recognised this, and repeatedly did battle against what he was convinced were unjust attacks upon Italy's attitude at the conference. It was in pursuance of his wish that in the Reichstag in November, 1906, I combated the reproaches that were cast upon Italy. Later, too, Herr von Radowitz expressed his opinion of the Italian delegates, to the following effect: that perhaps so far as appearances went they had been too anxious to place Franco-Italian relations in the most favourable light possible, but that in actual fact they had rendered us good service. The contrary opinion has just as little foundation as the widespread belief in Russia, that at the Berlin Congress Bismarck cheated and betrayed the Russians.

The Tripoli expedition gave the Italian nation opportunity for showing in a brilliant manner their patriotic solidarity and moral unity; but a section of our Press, especially at the beginning, judged it wrongly. Italy most certainly has interests that lie outside the sphere of the Triple Alliance. We ourselves have interests beyond the scope of Triple Alliance policy, and Austria does not lack them either. Prince Bismarck sharply emphasised this fact at times. The Triple Alliance would not have remained intact so long if it had demanded from the allied Powers absolute community in all their enterprises and in all the courses of their policy.

A well-known phrase, *"cum grano salis,"* and, by way of comparison, a fact of the internal political constitution of our State, may again be mentioned to characterise the Triple Alliance. Just as the German Empire gains in security and stability because its constitution, while requiring absolute obedience in all great national and political questions, leaves the single States free to deal with their own narrower problems, so the Triple Alliance unites the three Great Powers of Middle Europe on the great aim of Continental politics for which the Alliance was founded, but leaves them absolute freedom in the pursuit of their particular national interests. The existence of Italy, Austria, and Germany is rooted in European politics, and their roots are many and firmly intertwined. But the branches of the trees must be able to spread freely in every direction. The Triple Alliance must not and cannot act as the shears which check free growth without cogent reason.

There are politicians who refuse to estimate at its true value Italy's participation in the Triple Alliance. Their hesitation arises from a doubt as to whether Italy would be able and willing to go hand in hand with Austria and us in every possible complication of international politics. Even if these fears were justified, which is clearly not the case in view of the loyalty of the authorities in Italy, and of the political wisdom of the Italian nation, this would not be an argument against the value of Italy's participation in the Triple Alliance. Supposing Italy were not able in every conceivable circumstance to go to all lengths with Austria and us, and if we and Austria likewise were not able to support Italy in all complications of international politics, even then each one of the three Powers would, by virtue of the existing alliance, be prevented from assisting the enemy. That is what Prince Bismarck meant when he once remarked that it was sufficient for him that an Italian corporal with the Italian flag and a drummer beside him should array themselves against the West, i. e. France, and not against the East, i. e. Austria.

In the event of a dispute in Europe everything else depends on how the question is put, with what military force we are prepared to defend our view, and with what success our military and diplomatic efforts are crowned. The full and true value of an alliance can only be tested in a grave crisis. In times of peace the Triple Alliance is held together by such solid, almost indestructible interests in the sphere of Continental politics, that momentary and transitory disturbances in international matters cannot injure it seriously.

The Triple Alliance as a guarantee of peace has proved its worth for thirty years, and this justifies our hopes.

TURKEY.

The Bosnian question and the Tripoli affair, in which Austria and Italy were ranged against Turkey, who is on friendly terms with us, were not able to weaken the Triple Alliance. We have carefully cultivated good relations with Turkey and Islam, especially since the journey to the East undertaken by our Emperor and Empress. These relations are not of a sentimental nature, for the continued existence of Turkey serves our interest from the industrial, military, and political points of view. Industrially and financially, Turkey offered us a rich and fertile field of activity, to which Rodbertus and Friedrich List had already drawn attention, and which we have cultivated with much profit. In the undesired but possible event of a general European war, the military strength of Turkey might have been exerted in our favour. For our Austrian ally, Turkey was the most convenient neighbour possible. The introduction of our last Army Bill which had its origin in the change of situation effected by the Balkan War, shows that Turkey's collapse was a blow to us. I never had any illusions about the limits of Turkish ability to act with effect. For that very reason I strove, for many years successfully, to prevent any serious conflict in the Near East. In 1897, during the Cretan affair, in 1908-09, during the crisis caused by the annexation of Bosnia, and in all phases of the Macedonian question, there was great danger that serious trouble in the Balkan Peninsula would have more unfavourable than favourable results for us, as well as for Austro-Hungary, and would not make the European situation any easier for us to deal with. For many a year Turkey was a useful and important link in the chain of our political relations.

For the present our position in the Triple Alliance will remain the chief feature of our Foreign policy. The Triple Alliance has gained in value for us, partly because, owing to our growing share in international politics, and to the increase of our Navy, friction between England and Germany has considerably increased, and partly because of the change in the international situation brought about by the conclusion of the Franco-Russian Alliance.

RUSSIA.

Friendly relations with the Empire of the Tsars was a legacy bequeathed to the new German Empire by Prussia. Russia and Prussia have hardly ever been antagonists, if we except the time of the Empress Elizabeth's hatred of Frederick the Great, a hatred based on personal rather than material grounds, and of the mock war between Russia and Prussia in 1812.

The difficult task of dividing Poland certainly gave rise to some temporary friction, but it did not result in any serious conflict of views. Indeed, the Polish affair often brought Russia and Prussia into closer touch. The possibility of danger from Poland is a warning to both these countries not to quarrel, but to look on their common efforts to ward off attempts at re-establishing the independence of Poland as a bridge on which Russia and Prussia can continue to meet.

During the first half of the nineteenth century the relations between the ruling houses of Russia and Prussia were more intimate than is usual; and this intimacy found expression in the policy of the two countries. In the dark times of the Crimean War Prussia's friendly attitude considerably eased Russia's position; and a counterpart to this is found in the attitude which the Emperor Alexander II. adopted during the Franco-German War. Not long after the Peace of Frankfurt was signed, in September, 1872, the Emperors of Russia and Austria went to the capital of the new German Empire to visit the venerable sovereign who had emerged victorious from the great struggle. On this occasion they met on friendly terms, and by that time Prince Bismarck had created a new basis for European policy. The united strength of the empires of Eastern Europe cooled the French nation's ardour for revenge; indeed, this union was an excellent guarantee of peace. Bismarck also expected that the closer connection of Russia with the conservative tendencies of Germany and Austria's Foreign policy would stem the tide of Panslavism which at that time was rapidly rising in Russia. As he expressed it: "Russia, the wild elephant, was to walk between the two tame elephants, Germany and Austria."

The Berlin Congress, 1878, occasioned a slight rift in the hitherto unbroken concord of the Powers of Eastern Europe. After the heavy losses of a long and unexpectedly difficult campaign, Russia, who had not cared to risk the occupation of Constantinople, had to submit in Berlin to considerable modifications of the Peace of San Stefano. These alterations in their essentials may be traced back to secret arrangements made by the St. Petersburg Cabinet with Austria before the war against Turkey, and with

England at the close of the armistice. The results of the Berlin Congress were hardly satisfactory from the point of view of the Russian people; and the Russian Press, which in the last decade had greatly strengthened its influence on public opinion, put all the blame on Prince Bismarck, the chairman of the Congress and its most distinguished member. The Russian Imperial Chancellor, Prince Gortschakov, whose personal relations with Prince Bismarck had become gradually more and more unfriendly, not only gave free rein to the Press, but discussed with a French journalist the idea of a Franco-Russian Alliance, though this, of course, at the time, was nothing more than an idea. When the Emperor Alexander II. also seemed to be yielding to anti-German influences, Bismarck, in 1879, concluded the treaty of alliance with Austro-Hungary, which became the basis of the Triple Alliance. After the conclusion of this alliance, the *Times* correspondent in Paris, M. de Blowitz, a very versatile man, said to me: "That is probably the best stroke of diplomacy that Bismarck has yet achieved."

Nevertheless Prince Bismarck, with his accustomed energy, set to work to place us once more on our old footing with Russia. He succeeded in materially improving Russo-German relations, and, what is more, the meeting of the three Emperors at Skierniewice, in 1884, led to a new *rapprochement* of the three Empires. European peace was assured in an almost ideal fashion by the Triple Alliance on the one hand and the *entente* of the Powers of Eastern Europe on the other. But from the very first a limit was set to this ideal state of affairs by the many antagonistic aims of Russian and Austrian policy in the east. It was only a question of time that this antagonism should become manifest, for it did not depend on the goodwill or illwill of statesmen, but on the differences in the very real political interests of the two Empires. It was the Bulgarian question which again upset the good relations between Austria and Russia. The friendly understanding of the three Empires did not survive the stormy summer of 1886. It is well-known that Prince Bismarck himself declared that in the face of the new situation he had done his best, while remaining loyal to the Triple Alliance, to preserve a friendly understanding between Germany and Russia. To this end he had assured a more or less exceptional position for German policy behind the

defensive position of the Triple Alliance, by means
of the so-called Reinsurance Treaty with Russia.
Later on he spoke frequently and in detail about the
motives that had induced him to conclude the treaty,
and about the value and bearing of the same. He
blamed his successor for not renewing the treaty, and
he pointed out that it was after this failure to renew
that the Franco-Russian Alliance was concluded.
Russia, no longer bound by any convention, and
France in her isolation had joined forces, after the
dividing wall between them had been removed.
Prince Bismarck considered this change on the part
of Russia, from the side of the German Empire to
that of the bitterest enemy of Germany, a great
strengthening of France's position among the Powers, and one which would materially increase the difficulties of German policy.

THE FRANCO-RUSSIAN ALLIANCE.

At any rate the Franco-Russian Alliance denotes
a very significant change in the international situation. In the 'nineties we Germans had to face British
rivalry, roused by the rapid development of German
foreign trade and the construction of the German
fleet, while we were taken in the rear by the Dual

Alliance, by which France desired to profit as much as possible in order to realise her hopes.

Thus placed, we had to seek and find a means of transition to an international policy. At first this was a narrow path along which we had to advance with great care. Our attitude towards Russia during the Russo-Japanese War, was modelled on our relations with England during the Boer War. Without injuring Japan by failing in strictly proper neutrality, we adopted a very friendly attitude towards Russia. Indeed, our neutrality with respect to Russia was even a shade more kindly than that of France.

After the Russo-Japanese War there was a slight coolness in Franco-Russian relations, whereas there was an increase of warmth in those between Russia and Germany. The Dual Alliance had gradually lost a great deal of its original keenness of edge, not so much on account of the weakening of Russia, which, as was the case after the Crimean War, was often exaggerated, as on account of the restoration of confidence between Russia and Germany. The various stages of this re-establishment of friendly relations were marked by the repeated meetings between monarchs of the two Empires. After the Bosnian crisis, too, normal relations between Russia and Ger-

many were quickly restored, as was proved by the
particularly satisfactory meeting between the Emperor William and the Tsar, which took place
amongst the islands off the coast of Finland in June,
1909. It did not lie in Germany's power to separate
Russia from France, nor could she harbour any intention of so doing. Since a treaty of alliance has
been concluded between Russia and France, and has
penetrated the national sentiments of the two peoples, it has become impossible, and will for some time
to come continue to be impossible, for us to sever the
ties of this alliance, and bind Russia to our interests
by means of a treaty.

But Germany can blunt the keen edge of the Dual
Alliance by putting her relations with Russia on a
sound basis. It was possible to accomplish this task,
and it has been done. Its accomplishment was rendered considerably easier by the personal relations
subsisting between our Emperor and the Emperor
Nicholas. The hopes built by the French chauvinists
on the Russian Alliance have not been fulfilled. At
times Russian statesmen have even given France to
understand that Russia was not willing to serve the
cause of the French policy of revenge. The high
hopes with which the French acclaimed the conclusion

of the Dual Alliance have gradually faded. The
French authorities were forced to seek some compensation for their disappointed hopes, for the sake of
the sentiments and aspirations which ultimately control public feeling in France. They found this compensation in the Anglo-French *entente,* which at
times seemed a greater menace to us than the Dual
Alliance. The resentment of the French against the
rulers of Alsace-Lorraine sought and found an ally
in the widespread disquietude and jealousy of the
English, which increased in proportion as our navy
grew and our oversea interests developed.

The Dual Alliance completely lacks any permanent
interests hostile to the German Empire which are
common to the two Powers. There is probably no
European Power which so rarely stands in the way
of Russia's claims in the spheres of politics and industry as Germany. Conflicting interests between
England and France are certainly not wanting either.
Up to quite recent times England's greatest and most
important acquisitions in the wider world were made
at the expense of France; this was the case in the
Sudan, and earlier in Further India. But for
France oversea politics are not vital, and therefore
she was at liberty to subordinate her international in-

terests to England's, thereby circumscribing Franco-British differences for the sake of an Anglo-French agreement. France paid this high price for England's friendship after she had been disappointed in her hopes of the Dual Alliance.

GERMANY AND FRANCE.

The resentment against Germany might well be called the soul of French policy; the other international questions are more of a material nature and only concern the body. It is a peculiarity of the French nation that they place spiritual needs above material ones.

The irreconcilability of France is a factor that we must reckon with in our political calculations. It seems to me weakness to entertain the hope of a real and sincere reconciliation with France, so long as we have no intention of giving up Alsace-Lorraine. And there is no such intention in Germany. There certainly are many individual points in which we can see eye to eye with France, and in which we can co-operate, at any rate, from time to time. We must always endeavour to preserve polite, calm, and peaceful relations with France. But beyond that we should not pursue any will-o'-the-wisp delusions, otherwise we may meet with the fate of the Astronomer in La Fontaine, who, while gazing at the stars, fell into the pit which lay at his feet, but which he had not seen. In this case the pit is called *"Le trou des Vosges."*

Also, as regards France, we must not hope too much from attentions and amenities; the small change of international intercourse. In saying this we do homage to the proud patriotism of a great nation. The resentment against Germany lies too deep in the hearts of the French for us to be able to overcome it by cheap expressions of friendship. France was never so hard hit, not even after the catastrophic defeats of 1812–15, as by the war of 1870–71. In France there is no comprehension of the fact that what seems to them the brutal severity of a conqueror was really a matter of national necessity to us Germans. Perhaps in course of time the French nation will grow reconciled to the decisions of the Peace of Frankfurt, when it realises that they were and are irrevocable. But so long as France thinks she perceives a possibility of winning back Alsace-Lorraine, either by her own unaided efforts or with the help of others, so long will she consider the existing arrangement provisional and not final.

The French have the right to claim understanding for this feeling with which the majority of the people are deeply imbued. It is a proof of a lively sense of honour, if a nation suffers so keenly from a single injury to its pride that the desire for retribution becomes the ruling passion of the people. It is quite true that for many centuries France was responsible for the spirit of unrest which troubled the history of Europe. We had to fortify our position in the West in an enduring manner, so as to safeguard our peace from fresh disturbances. The remedy has not been altogether unavailing, not only so far as Germany is concerned, but for the whole of Europe. But the French see things in a different light. The policy of splendid adventures, which often has cost Europe its peace, and has repeatedly forced France's neighbours to strain their powers to the utmost, has made the past of France a record of glory, by which the peculiar national ambition of the French has found expression in the grandest and most spontaneous fashion. French history differs from the German in this point, among many others: that the greatest and most dramatic moments in which the fate of nations is decided are found in the story of her wars of conquest, whereas the most glorious pages of German history tell of deeds of national defence. We wish to prevent the return of such times as those of Louis XIV. and of Napoleon I., and for our greater security have therefore strengthened our frontiers against France; but it is just such times as these for which many Frenchmen long, and which in moments of excitement are the goal of the desires of the whole nation. Germany, deriving new vigour as she did from the events of 1866 and 1870, has devoted all her strength to the enlargement of her own national life. Every time the national powers of France were fortified she proceeded to acts of aggression abroad, and would do so again if she foresaw the likelihood of success.

We must take this into account, and consider that we ourselves should be the opponent against whom France would first turn if she thought that she could carry out a victorious campaign against Germany. The policy of revenge is supported by the unshakable belief of the French in the indestructibility of the vital power of France. This belief is based on all the experiences of French history. No nation has ever recovered so quickly as the French from the effects of national disasters; none have ever so easily regained their elasticity, their self-confidence and their energy, after grievous disappointments and apparently crushing defeats. More than once France appeared to be finally overcome by her enemies abroad, and so shattered by chaotic conditions at home, that Europe believed she had ceased to be dangerous. But always within a very short time the French nation confronted Europe in all its old strength, or even with added might, and was able again to take up the struggle for European supremacy, to threaten the balance of power once more.

The rise and fall of this nation has always astonished the States of Europe anew. The gradual decline from the proud height to which Louis XIV. had raised France seemed to be leading to the disintegration of the French State by the great Revolution, which was quickly followed by civil war, the disbandment of the army, the destruction of the old industrial prosperity, and the bankruptcy of the State. Ten years after the outbreak of the Revolution, the armies of the French Republic were masters of Italy, the Netherlands, and all the land west of the Rhine, and had penetrated victoriously into the heart of Germany; another ten years, and the first Empire was at the height of its glory and Napoleon seemed very near the attainment of his goal—dominion over the whole Continent. Then followed the disasters of Leipzig and Waterloo, the complete defeat of France, and twice in succession, the taking of her capital.

During more than twenty years of uninterrupted warfare, the French nation had drained to the dregs its industrial and physical resources; and yet under the second Empire France was able once more to rise to the foremost position. The consequences of the defeat of 1870 dealt France a more grievous blow than any previously. But it did not prevent this wonderfully elastic nation from rising yet again. What Alexis de Tocqueville said more than half a century ago about the French people in his classical work, "L'Ancien Régime et la Révolution," is in many respects still true to-day:

"Quand je considère cette nation en elle-même, je la trouve plus extraordinaire qu'aucun des événements de son histoire. En a-t-il jamais paru sur la terre une seule qui fût si remplie de contrastes et si extrême en chacun de ses actes, plus conduite par des sensations moins par des principes; faisant ainsi toujours plus mal ou mieux qu'on ne s'y attendait, tantôt au-dessous du niveau commun de l'humanité, tantôt fort au-dessus; un peuple tellement inaltérable dans

ses principaux instincts qu'on le reconnaît encore dans
des portraits qui ont été faits de lui il y a deux ou
trois mille ans, et en même temps tellement mobile dans
ses pensées journalières et dans ses goûts qu'il finit
par se devenir un spectacle inattendu à lui-même,
et demeure souvent aussi surpris que les étrangers
à la vue de ce qu'il vient de faire; le plus casanier et
le plus routinier de tous quand on l'abandonne à lui-
même, et lorsqu'une fois on l'a arraché malgré lui à
son logis et à ses habitudes, prêt à tout pousser
jusqu'au bout du monde et à tout oser; indocile par
tempérament, et s'accomodant mieux toutefois de
l'empire arbitraire et même violent d'un prince que
du gouvernement régulier et libre des principaux
citoyens; aujourd'hui l'ennemi déclaré de toute obéis-
sance, demain mettant à servir une sorte de passion
que les nations les mieux douées pour la servitude ne
peuvent atteindre; conduit par un fil tant que per-
sonne ne résiste, ingouvernable dès que l'exemple de
la résistance est donné quelque part; trompant toujours ainsi ses maîtres, qui le craignent ou trop ou trop
peu; jamais si libre qu'il faille désespérer de l'asservir,
ni si asservi qu'il ne puisse encore briser le joug; apte
à tout, mais n'excellant qua dans la guerre; adorateur
du hasard, de la force, du succès, de l'éclat et du bruit,

plus que de la vraie gloire; plus capable d'héroïsme
que de vertu, de génie que de bon sens, propre à con-
cevoir d'immenses desseins plutôt qu' à parachever de
grandes entreprises; la plus brillante et la plus dange-
reuse des nations de l'Europe, et la mieux faite pour
y devenir tour à tour un objet d'admiration, de haine,
de pitié, de terreur, mais jamais d'indifférence?" *

* "When I contemplate this nation itself, it strikes me as more extraordinary than any of the events in its history. Was there ever in this
world a people so full of contrasts, so extreme in each one of its actions,
more guided by emotions and less by principles? Thus always doing better or worse than was expected, at one time below the common level of
humanity, at another far above it; a people so stable in their principal
instincts that they are still recognisable in portraits that were drawn
two or three thousand years ago, and at the same time so changeable in
their daily thoughts and in their tastes, that they themselves are finally
astonished at the spectacle they present, and are often as surprised as
foreigners at the sight of what they have just done; the most stay-at-
home creatures of habit when left to themselves, but once they have
been forced, against their will, to abandon their accustomed dwellings
and uses, ready to carry all before them to the ends of the earth, and to
dare anything; intractable by nature, and nevertheless submitting with a
better grace to the arbitrary and even brutal rule of a prince, than to the
orderly and free government of the principal citizens; one day the
avowed enemy of all allegiance, the next day serving with such a passionate devotion as even the nations most prone to servitude cannot attain;
people who can be guided by a thread as long as no one resists, but who
become ungovernable as soon as the example to resist is given anywhere;
thus always deceiving their masters who fear them either too little or too
much; never so free that it is hopeless to try and subjugate them, nor
so utterly enslaved that they cannot throw off the yoke; qualified for
anything, but excelling only in war; worshipping chance, force, success,
show and clamour, rather than true glory; more capable of heroism than
of virtue, of genius than of common sense, better able to conceive im-

It is a fact that very soon after the re-establishment of her political system, which, as after every
military disaster, had been overthrown as a result of
the defeats of Wörth and Sedan, France, whose
activity in the field of continental politics had been
paralysed for the time being, exerted her power with
much effect in the sphere of world-politics. In the
course of the last twenty-five years she has founded
a colonial empire that much more than compensates
her for the loss of land and population she suffered
in Europe, and has thus raised herself to the position
of the second greatest colonial Power in the world.
Her possessions in North Africa, which lie at her very
gates, have been nearly doubled by the acquisition of
Morocco.

This is not the place to discuss whether, as many
think, the complete and unlimited control of Morocco
in political, industrial and military matters will be a
source of weakness, or whether it will not rather lend
added strength to France. In any case, the colonial
activity of France proves how quickly and vigorously
the French spirit of enterprise revived soon after the

mense schemes than to consummate great undertakings; the most brilliant and the most dangerous of the nations of Europe, and the most
apt to become in turn an object of admiration, hatred, pity and terror,
but never one of indifference."

defeat of 1870, and attempted to win national ascendancy in the path which lay open, and which Germany
had designedly left open in Tunis and in Tonquin.

But France will not look upon her great colonial
empire as a sufficient compensation for the loss of
Alsace-Lorraine.   And Bismarck had no illusions on
this point when he recommended us to promote the
success of France's colonial policy in order to distract
the attention of the French, at any rate temporarily,
from the neighbourhood of the Vosges.

THE MOROCCO QUESTION.

When we fell out with France on the Morocco
question, it was not our object to thwart her colonial
policy, but we had weighty interests of our own as
well as our national reputation to defend.   Our action in the Moroccan affair had its legal justification
in the Treaty of Madrid of 1880, and the German-
Moroccan Commercial Treaty of 1890.   We were
driven to take such action by the high-handed policy
of France in Morocco, which threatened to ignore
German industrial and commercial interests as well
as our national credit.

The Moroccan Treaty, concluded in Madrid in
1880, had defined the European Powers' right to ex-

ercise protection over Morocco. It was concluded on the basis of the recognition of the sovereign rights of Morocco. On the strength of this basis Germany concluded a commercial treaty with Morocco in 1890. No change in the arrangements made at Madrid was valid without the assent of the signatory Powers— namely, the Great Powers of Europe with the exception of Russia, the United States, the Scandinavian States, Holland, Belgium and Portugal. France certainly had a special interest in the development of affairs in Morocco, which adjoins one of her own colonial possessions. This fact was always taken into account by Germany. On the basis of the arrangements made at Madrid, no objection could have been taken to the special consideration of the particular interests of France and Spain. But French wishes went far beyond this. France interfered more and more unscrupulously in Moroccan affairs. She hoped, by ignoring the Treaty of Madrid, and disregarding the economic interests of other countries, especially those of Germany, quietly to acquire a large new colonial possession of great value. In the pursuit of this policy France relied on England, assuming that the support and countenance of that country was sufficient to enable her to attain her ends.

On April 8, 1904, a separate treaty was made between England and France, in which France acknowledged England's undisputed authority in Egypt, and England expressed her approval of France's action in Morocco. This separate treaty disregarded, with an equal lack of ceremony, both the International Settlement of 1880 and the German-Moroccan Commercial Treaty. As one of the first tangible results of the Anglo-French *entente,* which was indirectly antagonistic to Germany, this treaty obviously aimed at injuring the latter country.

The two Powers disposed arrogantly of a great and most important field of colonial interests, without even deigning to take the German Empire into consideration. It was clearly an attempt on the part of the Western Powers to lay claim to the right of decision in matters of international policy. The French authorities did not hesitate to act immediately upon the Anglo-French arrangement, as if the signatory Powers of the Treaty of Madrid had no existence at all. France set about the "Tunification" of Morocco. The French agent in Morocco, St. Réné-Taillandier, tried to secure a share in the government of the country. By altering the police organisation, by founding a National Bank under French direction, and by entrusting public works and contracts to French firms, the industrial life and government in Morocco were to be brought under French influence to such an extent that the ultimate annexation of Morocco as a French possession would have been merely a matter of form. The Minister for Foreign Affairs at that time—Delcassé, a most gifted and energetic statesman, but too easily swayed by his feelings where Germany was concerned —cherished the hope of confronting us with a *fait accompli* in Morocco. He knew that in so doing he would deal our prestige in the world a severe blow. We had important and promising economic interests in Morocco which were seriously injured by French action. In addition to this, our dignity and our newly-won position in international politics were at stake. The fact that the signatory Powers of the Treaty of Madrid had been ignored in the Anglo-French Moroccan arrangement was equivalent *in specie* to an affront to the German Empire. France had made a friendly treaty with England, secret negotiations were being carried on with Spain, Russia was not a signatory Power, Italy went her own way in the Mediterranean, the affairs of Morocco were of little interest to the United States, and there was no reason to expect serious opposition from the smaller States of Europe. Thus only Austria and, above all, Germany were clearly set aside. A weighty choice lay before us. Should we allow ourselves to be left out, and treated as a *quantité négigeable,* in an important international decision? Or should we demand that our interests be considered and our wishes consulted? The first course would have been the easier; we were urged to adopt the second, not only by our sense of honour and our pride, but also by our interests, rightly interpreted. If once we suffered ourselves to be trampled on with impunity, this first attempt to treat us badly would soon have been followed by a second and a third.

On July 3, 1900, the Emperor William II. had given utterance to the words: "I am not of opinion that our German people, under the leadership of their princes, conquered and suffered thirty years ago in order to be set aside in important decisions on foreign affairs. If this should happen, the German nation's position as a world-Power would be destroyed for good and all, and I do not wish this to come to pass." French Moroccan policy was an obvious attempt to set Germany aside in an important decision on foreign affairs, an attempt to adjust the balance of power in Europe in favour of France. A precedent would have been established which must of necessity have tempted to repetition. We could not risk that. From this point of view the Moroccan affair became a national question for us. The course of our policy in Morocco was clearly indicated.

On March 31, 1905, His Majesty the Emperor, in pursuance of my advice, landed at Tangier, where he defended the independence and sovereignty of Morocco in unequivocal language. The demands of Germany to be consulted about Moroccan affairs were thus announced to the world. It was made clear that Germany intended to adhere to the international treaty of 1880, based on the acknowledgment of the sovereignty of Morocco, and that she was not inclined to recognise the new situation created without her consent by the Anglo-French Moroccan Treaty and the action of France in that country. Our object was to substitute an international settlement by the signatory Powers of the Treaty of Madrid for the one-sided arrangement between England and France. We also had to prevent an international conference from simply giving its consent to French policy in Morocco. Both ends were attained by the fact that the Conference of Algeciras actually took place, and by the decisions it made. France violently opposed the scheme of calling a conference. For a time it seemed as if M. Delcassé would make the question of peace or war depend on this point. When the German government refused to yield, France consented to the conference. M. Delcassé resigned the portfolio of Foreign Affairs. He retired, and we got our way because we stood firm. In Algeciras our position was naturally a difficult one, seeing that we were opposed to the Powers of the *entente,* and that the other Powers took little interest in the Moroccan question. Nevertheless we succeeded in preserving the sovereignty of the Sultan and in securing international control of the police organisation and the Moroccan National Bank, thus ensuring the open door in Morocco for German economic interests as well as for those of all other countries. We did not attain all we wished, but at least all that was essential. We had foiled the attempt to set us aside in the settlement of an affair of great international importance. We should have a voice in the further development of Moroccan affairs, and we did not need to renounce our right to this without adequate compensation. The decisions of the Algeciras Conference bolted the door against the attempts of France to compass the "Tunification" of Morocco. They also provided a bell we could ring at any time should France show any similar tendencies again. Very soon after the Algeciras Conference the new state of affairs made itself felt in a painful manner in France. The "nefarious Algeciras document" was characterised as "European tutelage forced upon France," or at best as an "honourable retreat." It has been said that after the resignation of Delcassé we ought to have tried to come to a direct understanding with France. It is a question whether France was at all inclined to pay us an acceptable price. Any way, it was not open to us to pursue this course, if only on account of our position with regard to Turkey and Islam. In November, 1898, the Emperor William II. had said in Damascus: "The three hundred million Mahommedans who live scattered over the globe may be assured of this, that the German Emperor will be their friend at all times." In Tangier the Emperor had declared emphatically in favour of the integrity of Morocco. We should have completely destroyed our credit in the Mahommedan world, if so soon after these declarations we had sold Morocco to the French. Our Ambassador in Constantinople, Freiherr von

Marschall, said to me at the time: "If we sacrifice Morocco in spite of Damascus and Tangier, we shall at one fell swoop lose our position in Turkey, and therefore all the advantages and prospects that we have painfully acquired by the labour of many years."

The separate Franco-German Treaty of February 9, 1909, which was concluded with the distinguished assistance of von Kiderlen-Wächter, later Secretary of State diminished the likelihood of continual friction between the two countries. It secured France a certain amount of political influence without making annexation possible; but it retained the principle of the open door, and it afforded German and French commerce and industry equal rights in the State of Morocco, which preserved its independence without loss of territory. The arrangement promoted peace in that it supplemented the Algeciras settlement in such points as had proved in practice to require correction. The decisions of the Algeciras Conference were explicitly confirmed by the treaty of 1909. The German right to a voice in decisions touching the fate of Morocco, this right which stood in the way of the annexation of the country by France, was in no way affected by the separate treaty. What we received later in return for renouncing this right—whether it

be much or little, whether the piece of land in the
Congo that fell to our share be of great value or small
—was certainly obtained on the basis of the Algeciras
decisions, and thanks to our action in the year 1905.
We never had any intention of taking possession of
any part of Morocco; not because we were afraid of
France, but for our own sake. England and Spain,
besides France, would have opposed us there. On the
other hand, we could not hope to reconcile France
by exaggeratedly friendly advances in the Moroccan
question. However high the economic value that
France sets upon Morocco, however great the increase
of power which she expects from this addition to her
North African possessions, her Moroccan policy was
—especially at critical moments—rather a means to
an end than an end in itself. In certain French
circles the original object was to ignore Germany,
and thus, with the help of England, to make an effective attack on our position and credit in the world;
later on they thought they saw a chance, with the support of England, to come to a final settlement with
Germany under most favourable conditions. These
tendencies of French policy twice brought the Morocco question into the van of international politics
and endangered the peace of the world.

THE IRRECONCILABILITY OF FRANCE.

When we consider our relations with France, we must not forget that she is unappeased. So far as man can tell, the ultimate aim of French policy for many years to come will be to create the necessary conditions, which to-day are still wanting, for a settlement with Germany with good prospects of success. If we soberly realise this truth, we shall be able to adopt a proper attitude towards France. Indignant tirades against the incorrigibility of the French are in very bad taste, as are futile attempts to propitiate them. The German "Michel" has no need again and again to approach the coy beauty with flowers in his hand; her gaze is riveted on the Vosges. Only an acceptance of the irrevocability of the loss of 1871 can accustom France finally and without restriction to the state of affairs fixed in the Peace of Frankfurt. It is just possible that the effect of convulsively straining her military resources to the uttermost may, by reacting on the economic and social conditions of France, hasten the return of pacific feelings, and that once again the French proverb may prove true, "*Que l'excès du mal amène la guérison.*" The reintroduction of military service for a period of three years betokens such a rise in the "armament fever," that it may lead to the return of a normal temperature. Should the three-year military service entail an income tax, this would also probably have a sobering effect.

Till such time France will be against us. Although she is at great pains to remedy the military disadvantage at which she stands in comparison with our State, and which is due to her smaller population, she no longer has the old-time confidence in her proper strength. It is the aim of French policy, by means of alliances and friendships, to restore the balance between France and her German neighbour, or even, if possible, to turn the scales in her own favour. To this end France has had to renounce a part of her own free initiative, and has become more dependent than formerly on foreign Powers. The French, of course, are very well aware of this. The fact that the hyper-sensitive national pride of the French acquiesces in this shows what is the predominant desire of the people. It is hardly possible to imagine any international situation which could induce France to change fundamentally the policy inspired by the memory of 1870.

When, shortly after the Krüger telegram, enthusiasm for the Boers ran high in France, as in all Europe, an English Minister anxiously asked a French diplomat whether France might not be tempted to side with Germany. The Frenchman's answer ran as follows: "You may rest assured that as long as Alsace-Lorraine remains German, whatever else may happen, the French nation will consider Germany its permanent enemy, and will regard any other Power merely as an accidental opponent."

FASHODA.

The course and the result of the quarrel about Fashoda showed how little success or failure in the wider world count in the estimation of France, when compared with her loss of position in Europe. France suffered an undeniable defeat in this quarrel with England, and this was keenly felt. Fashoda stood for the end of an old and proud dream of French colonial policy, and made the French nation feel the superiority of British power in a pitiless fashion.

For a moment public opinion in France was enraged and turned impetuously against England. The bulk of those people who in politics cannot distinguish between the transitory and the permanent, and mistake the noisy din of actuality for the echo of what is really significant, thought that a change had come over French policy. The ill-feeling against England was to drive France to the side of Germany, the disappointment about their ill-success in the Sudan was to paralyse resentment at the loss of Alsace-Lorraine, and new hope of requital for Fashoda was to take the place of the old hope of revenge for Metz and Sedan. It was impossible to misunderstand the nature of French policy more thoroughly than by imagining such a state of affairs. A nation that for a whole generation has cherished one hope and one ideal will not turn aside from its old course because of a misadventure on a remote track. The hatred of Germany could not be affected, let alone removed, by ill-feeling against England. Even if the momentary anger against England had been far more passionate and heartfelt than it actually was, it would, nevertheless, not have been the beginning of permanently hostile feelings, for the attitude of France to England had been definitely established in French policy before the trouble in the Sudan. France soon discovered in English jealousy of Germany her natural ally against the victor of 1870, and pressed to England's side. There was disappointment in Paris because England would not, for the sake of French friendship, sacrifice any of her interests in the Sudan and on the Nile, but France was ready in any case, though with clenched teeth, to pay this price, or even a higher one, for England's friendship. The defeat in the Fashoda affair was set down in the debit account of the French policy of revenge, and finally resulted in renewed hatred of Germany rather than in hostility towards England. Forty-eight hours after France had yielded in the Fashoda affair, a French ambassador, one of the best political intellects of France, was asked by an Italian colleague what effect this event would have on French relations with England. The Frenchman replied: "An excellent one! Once the difference about the Sudan is settled nothing stands in the way of a complete *entente* with England."

THE TRIPLE ENTENTE.

This *entente* really became an accomplished fact not long after the Fashoda incident, and has persisted through all the changes of international politics. Owing to her alliance with France, and the complications in the East, Russia has often supported the Anglo-French *entente,* so that we are justified in speaking of a Triple *entente* as a counterpart to the Triple Alliance.

The political leadership of this triple union has, at
decisive moments, mostly been in the hands of England, and up till now England, like Russia, has refused to serve the cause of French revenge.   She has
been guided mainly by her own interests.   English
leadership has sometimes made our life difficult, but
just as often it has had a soothing and sobering effect
on France, and has done excellent work for the preservation of peace in Europe.

GERMANY—FRANCE—ENGLAND.

England is certainly seriously disquieted by our
rising power at sea, and our competition which incom-
modes her at many points.   Without doubt there are
still Englishmen who think that, on the principle expressed by Montaigne, "que le dommage de l'un est
le profit de l'autre," that if the troublesome German
would disappear from the face of the earth, England
would only gain by it.   But between such sentiments
in England and the fundamental feeling in France,
there is a marked difference, which finds corresponding expression in politics.   France would attack us
if she thought she were strong enough; England
would only do so if she thought she could not defend
her vital economic and political interests against Ger-

many except by force. The mainspring of English policy towards us is national egoism; that of French policy is national idealism. He who follows his interest will, however, mostly remain calmer than he who pursues an idea.

ANGLO-GERMAN SETTLEMENT.

Doubtless the English merchant has at times been irked by the competition abroad of his German colleague; doubtless German and English economic interests do clash here and there in the world. But in the course of her great world-policy, England has hardly found any Great Power bar her way less often then the German Empire. This fact has not escaped the English, in spite of their anxiety about the German navy. Germany and England are probably the only two great European Powers who have never shed a drop of each other's blood. There has been friction and tension between them, but never war. Happily in England, too, the conviction is gaining ground that England, by continually opposing Germany and by overdoing the anti-German policy, only injures herself. Finally, this greatest of commercial nations knows very well what excellent customers Germany and England are of each other, and how grievously British industrial life would feel the loss of German custom. If, on the one hand, there are many opposing interests in Germany and England, on the other they have very vital interests in common. And, in truth, the danger to English supremacy at sea in the new world and sea power belongs only to the sphere of possibilities—or rather of imagination—and not to the realm of tangible realities.

The attitude of England to Germany is really not comparable with that of France to us. France moves in a circle round the thought of Alsace-Lorraine. English policy is no doubt influenced by the widespread uneasiness due to Germany's industrial expansion and growing sea power. But since the end of the policy of isolation in the year 1908, England no longer thinks of making her whole international policy, or every detail of her relations with Germany, dependent on her antagonism to us. Although, since we first trod the path of international politics, we have often found England opposed to us, yet now that we have attained the necessary power of defence at sea, our relations with England can be amicable and friendly. Rightly recognising that peace and friendship between Germany and England are beneficial to both countries, and that enmity and strife are equally disadvantageous for both, the Emperor William II., since his accession to power, has worked spontaneously and with never-failing zeal to restore friendly relations between the two great Germanic nations. There are many fields in which both have parallel interests. Whenever co-operation from which both parties derive advantage is possible, there is no reason why they should not go side by side and hand in hand. In proportion as the conviction spreads here and in England, that the national interests of both countries profit most by concerted action, the preliminary conditions for steadfast and honest trust and friendship will at last gain ground. The fact that the danger of an armed conflict between England and Germany seemed very imminent in the summer of 1911, by no means indicates that the struggle is only postponed and not terminated. It has often happened that diplomacy has come to the end of its peaceful resources and seemed obliged to leave further explanations to armed force. But the very imminence of this critical moment has often sufficed to give a fresh impetus to negotiations which had come to a standstill, and to bring about a peaceful solution— a solution which smooths away the dangerous differences, not only for the time being, but permanently.

War clouds are inevitable in the political sky. But the number of those that burst is far smaller than the number of those that disappear. Clouds equally heavy, if not heavier, threatened the peace between England and France in the 'forties of the last century, at the time of the July Monarchy, and also during the Second Empire. War seemed inevitable between England and Russia in 1885, when the Afghan question reached a critical point. All these threatening clouds melted away without bursting.

Our relations with England require particularly firm and steady handling. We desire amicable and even friendly relations with England, but we are not afraid of hostile ones. Official Germany and the nation itself must model their behaviour accordingly. A policy of running after England is as pointless as a policy of offensiveness. The English people, politically the maturest of the nations, would not be turned aside from any course they had once recognised as profitable by the warmest protestations of friendship; and in friendly acts that were not obviously inspired by interest they would see only a confession of our weakness. On the other hand, a proud and courageous nation like the English is not to be intimidated by threats, whether open or veiled. We confront England to-day, supported as we are by a navy which demands respect, in a very different manner from fifteen years ago, when it was a question of avoiding any conflict with England as long as possible, till we had built our fleet. At that time our foreign policy was, to a certain extent, regulated by the question of armaments; it had to be carried on under abnormal conditions. To-day the normal state of affairs is restored; our armaments are at the service of our policy. The friendship as well as the enmity of the German Empire, supported by a strong navy, are naturally matters of very much greater importance to England to-day than the friendship or enmity of Germany in the 'nineties, when she was unarmed at sea. The change in favour of Germany of the proportionate strength of the two countries, has relieved our foreign policy with regard to England of a great burden. We need no longer take such care to prevent England from injuring our safety and wounding our dignity; with our own unaided strength we are able, as is meet for Germans, to defend our dignity and our interests against England at sea, as we have for centuries defended them against the Continental Powers on land. We must look very far back in German history to find a like change in Germany's position in the world.

THE SUCCESSES OF GERMAN WORLD POLICY.

German policy, even before it had procured a strong navy, was able to secure points of support which promised well for our international interests in the future. We developed and improved our old colonial possessions. The serious rising of the Hereros in South-West Africa was put down, thanks to the endurance and courage of our troops, though it was at great expense and at the cost of grievous sacrifices. The names of the brave men who fought and died in the African desert—I will only mention Count Wolff-Werner von Arnim and Freiherr Burkhard von Erffa, who each went out as volunteers, and met death heroically there—deserve to live in our history, for they proved that our nation did not lose its military virtues during a long period of peace.

The South-West African rising marked a crisis in our colonial policy, but also a change for the better. By reorganising the Colonial Administration, by transforming the Colonial Department of the Foreign Ministry into an independent Imperial Ministry, and above all by arousing a lively comprehension of our tasks and aims in the colonies, we succeeded, at last, during the tenure of office of the Secretary of State, Herr Dernburg, in getting our colonial policy off the dead centre. It was just the same as with the navy. With great trouble, and after a long fight, we were at last lucky enough to convince all civil parties of the commonalty of the usefulness and necessity of a positive colonial policy, and to gain their support for such. About the time when we began to build our fleet, we established ourselves, in the autumn of 1897, in Kiau Chau, and a few months later we concluded the Shantung Treaty with China, which was one of the most significant actions in modern German history, and which secured for us a "place in the sun" in the Far East, on the shores of the Pacific Ocean, which have a great future before them.

Up to the end of the nineteenth century Europe had been able to work only on the outskirts of China. Since then the interior has been opened up more and more. There is much to be gained by introducing industries into a huge Empire, with a population of four hundred million, where the people are hard-working. We must not fall to the rear in this boundless field of action, but must consolidate and develop our position there. The end of the Spanish-American

War of 1899 gave us the opportunity to acquire the Caroline and Marianne Islands, and thus win a point of support in Polynesia. A year later we succeeded in bringing to an end the long quarrel over Samoa by a settlement with England and America that was to our advantage. In the year 1898 we concluded a treaty with England, which was significant, not only because, at a somewhat difficult stage our relations with England were made easier without endangering our position with regard to other Powers, but also because we secured thereby valuable prospects for the future. This treaty held out hopes of more profitable results the more patiently we waited till the time should arrive to realise them; it was brought about largely by the efforts of our ambassador in London at that time, Count Paul Hatzfeld, whom Bismarck used to call the best horse in his diplomatic stables. The Bagdad Railway scheme was a result of the Emperor's journey to Palestine, which he took in the autumn of 1898, a very few months after the first Navy Bill was passed, and which was in every respect so successful. This threw open to German influence and German enterprise a field of activity between the Mediterranean Sea and the Persian Gulf, on the rivers Euphrates and Tigris, and along their banks; this can hardly be surpassed for fertility and for its great possibilities of development in the future. If one can speak of boundless prospects anywhere, it is in Mesopotamia.

The German Empire to-day is a great World Power, not only by virtue of its industrial and commercial interests, but of its power in international politics; its power in the sense that its arm can reach to the farthest corners of the world, and that German interests can be injured nowhere with impunity. The sphere of German power has literally been extended over the whole world by the construction of our fleet, so that it can protect German interests scattered over the face of the earth. We built our navy as a means of national defence and to strengthen our national safety, and we have never used it for any other purpose.

The problem of modern German international politics, to secure a foundation for our position as a Great Power, on the whole may be considered to be solved. No doubt the German Empire was unwillingly accepted as a Great Power by those States which for centuries had been used to settling questions of oversea politics alone. But our right to a voice in international matters is recognised to-day in every country where the German flag is seen.   We had to reach this goal.   It was of the same significance as the creation of our navy, and could only be attained by overcoming considerable difficulties both in the sphere of foreign, or international, and of home, or national, politics.

During the first decade after the introduction of the Navy Bill of 1897, we had to pass through a zone of extreme danger in our foreign policy, for we were to provide ourselves with adequate sea power to protect our interests effectually, without at the time having sufficient strength at sea to defend ourselves. Germany has emerged from this critical period, unharmed and without loss of dignity or prestige.   In the autumn of 1897 the *Saturday Review* published that famous article, which culminated in the statement that, if Germany were swept off the face of the earth to-morrow, there would be no Englishman the day after but would be the richer for it, and ended with the words: *"Germaniam esse delendam."*

Twelve years later two important English newspapers, neither of them particularly pro-German, declared that the position of Germany was greater and stronger than at any time since the retirement of

Prince Bismarck.   From 1897 onward a significant development had taken place that was not always realised by contemporaries, but that posterity will recognise and appreciate.   During those years, by building our fleet, we accomplished the transition to international politics.   Our ascent into the regions of world-policy was successful.   We did not allow ourselves to be thrust forward by any Power against another, nor did we permit anyone to use us a catspaw.   By our calm bearing during the Boer War we took the first keen edge off the excitement which reigned in England after the Krüger telegram; and in the further course of events we gave England no cause to thwart us in the building of our fleet.   On the other hand, while we carefully cultivated the Triple Alliance, we never came into actual conflict with the Dual Alliance, which would have hindered us in the gradual acquirement of a navy.   What with the Anglo-French *Entente* and the Dual Alliance, we had to follow a narrow path which grew even narrower when the former expanded into a Triple *Entente,* and would have been impassable without extreme caution, when England surrounded us with a web of alliances and *ententes.*   When at last, during the Bosnian crisis, the sky of international politics cleared, when German power on the Continent burst its encompassing bonds, we had already got beyond the stage of preparation in the construction of our fleet.

THE IDEA OF A NAVY IN GERMANY.

Besides the difficulties of foreign politics there were the difficulties of home politics, though the latter were easier to overcome. We Germans have not the gift of meeting the demands of a new era cheerfully and spontaneously. Goethe pointed to the heart of our strength but also of our weakness when he said that it was characteristic of the Germans that they take everything heavily. The proverbial struggle between the old time and the new has suffered less interruption in the course of our history than in that of any other nation, and in every phase of any importance in our development it occurs again and again with undiminished strength. But, though amongst us innovations may have to encounter more vigorous opposition than elsewhere, yet in the end our development has never been impeded to such an extent as to cause lasting harm. We can even say that the uninterrupted continuance of antagonistic criticism has saved us Germans from dangerous innovations, and has brought us the steady ascent and sure progress in which we may rejoice to-day. That is what Bismarck meant when he said that rulers in Germany required the barbed wire of criticism, which kept them to the right path, because they ran the risk of tearing their hands to pieces if they engaged in movements that were too eccentric. Of course, Bismarck did not imply by this that criticism is always, or even mostly, in the right. But this spirit of negation forces men to show gravity, the strength of conviction, and the power of persuasion, and to be really clear in their minds as to the necessity of treading new paths. Wherever in Germany it has been possible to convince the majority of the people, including those who were at first antagonistic, of the necessity of a thing, we have found that this new conviction, though slowly acquired, has taken firm root.

All Germany to-day is imbued with the idea of the necessity of having a navy. From the most pronounced Agrarians among the Conservatives, to the extreme wing of the Democracy, there is no radical opposition to our German naval policy. The Ultra-Liberals, as is well known, had partly refused their support to the great, fundamental Navy Bills. They really and truly represented the antagonism of the old era to the new. It was in the year 1900 that, after a long and excited session of the Budget Committee, the leader of the people's party, Eugen Richter, came to me and said to me privately: "You will succeed, you will get a majority for your supplementary estimates for the Navy. I would never have believed it." In the interview that followed I was at pains to explain to this man, in many ways so distinguished, why his opposition to the Navy Bill was inexplicable to me, for the German democracy had for decades demanded German efficiency at sea. Herwegh stood at the cradle of the German fleet, and the first German warships had been built in 1848. I pointed out all the reasons why we must protect our commerce and our industries on the ocean. Richter listened attentively and said at last: "You may be right. But I am too old, I cannot take part in this new turn of affairs." The change prophesied by Eugen Richter was soon to be accomplished. The opposition of the people's party was based less on principle than on the general position of party politics. It was possible to overcome it in the course of party politics, and during the time of the Block it was overcome.

Prince Bismarck, the great and victorious man, who was the exact opposite of a leader of progress, bore striking and direct testimony to the recognition of the dawn of a new era.   A few years after the Prince's retirement that excellent general director, Herr Ballin, suggested that he should have a look at the Hamburg harbour, which Bismarck, in spite of its nearness to Friedrichsruh, had not visited for a long time.   After a tour round the harbour Herr Ballin took the eighty-year-old Prince on to one of the new trans-atlantic liners of the Hamburg-Amerika Company.   Prince Bismarck had never yet seen a ship of such dimensions.   He stopped when he set foot on the giant steamboat, looked at the ship for a long time, at the many steamers lying in the vicinity, at the docks and huge cranes, at the mighty picture presented by the harbour, and said at last: "I am stirred and moved.   Yes, this is a new age—a new world."   The mighty founder of the Empire, who fulfilled our national hopes and solved the problem of Germany's Continental policy, in his old age, with the never-failing insight of genius, recognised the future, the new tasks of the German Empire in the sphere of world-politics.

HOME POLICY

HOME POLICY

I

INTRODUCTION

THE history of our home policy, with the exception of a few bright spots, is a history of political mistakes. Despite the abundance of merits and great qualities with which the German nation is endowed, political talent has been denied it. No people has found it so difficult as the Germans to attain solid and permanent political institutions, although we were the first, after the downfall of antiquity and the troublous times of the migration of nations, to acquire that peace in national existence which is founded on might, and which is the preliminary condition for the growth of real political life. Though, thanks to our military prowess, we found it easy enough to overcome foreign obstruction and interference in our national life, at all times we found it very hard to overcome even small obstacles in our own political development.

It has often happened to other nations that military disasters, disasters in their foreign policy, have severely injured and even overthrown their form of government at home. We Germans, owing to our political clumsiness, have often defrauded ourselves of successes won in battle, and for centuries rendered an effective foreign policy impossible by our narrow-minded and short-sighted home policy.

We are not a political people. Not that we ever lacked penetration and understanding for the sequence of political things, or for the essence and association of the religious, moral, social, legal and industrial forces which condition politics. We have always possessed this political knowledge to the same extent as our contemporaries, and even to a greater. We did not either fail to realise our own peculiar political shortcomings. But what we did lack, and what we still often lack, is the art of proceeding from insight to practical application, and the greater art of doing the right thing, politically, by a sure creative instinct, instead of only after much thought and considerable cogitation.

How can it otherwise be explained that in the struggle between different nationalities the German has so often succumbed to the Czech and the Slovene, the Magyar and the Pole, the French and the Italian, and that he still is at a disadvantage to-day? That in this sphere he usually comes off second best in comparison with almost all his neighbours?

Politically, as in no other sphere of life, there is an obvious disproportion between our knowledge and our power. We can boast at present of a particularly flourishing state of political science and especially political economy. We shall seldom feel the influence of deep learning on practical politics. This is not because only a small class of educated men, and not the mass of the people, participate and take an interest in knowledge. The German nation, on the contrary, more than any other people, and particularly as regards the lower classes, is eager to learn and capable of so doing. Among many fine traits of character that is one of the finest our nation possesses. But for the German the knowledge of political things is usually a purely intellectual matter, which he does not care to connect with the actual occurrences of political life. It would be possible for him to do so only in the rarest cases. For, although well-developed logical powers result in good judgment, yet there is too often a lack of that political discernment which can grasp the bearing of acquired knowledge on the life of the community. The want of political aptitude sets a narrow limit, even to highly developed political science. During my term of office I took a lively interest in furthering political instruction, and I expect the results to be better and better the more Germans of all classes and all degrees of culture are given the opportunity of following such courses of instruction. But much water will flow under the bridges before these weaknesses and deficiencies in our political character, which are partly innate and partly acquired by education, can be so removed. In the meantime Fate, who, as we all know, is an excellent but expensive teacher, might undertake to educate us politically, and that by means of the injuries which our innate political failings must inflict on us again and again. Failings, even political ones, are seldom cured by knowledge, mostly only by experience. Let us hope that the experience, which shall enable us to acquire a political talent in addition to so many other fine gifts, will not be too painful an one. In spite of a past full of political disasters, we do not yet possess that talent. I once had a conversation on this subject with the late Ministerial Director Althoff. "Well, what can you expect?" replied that distinguished man in his humorous way. "We Germans are the most learned nation in the

world and the best soldiers. We have achieved great
things in all the sciences and arts; the greatest philosophers, the greatest poets and musicians are Germans.
Of late we have occupied the foremost place in the
natural sciences and in almost all technical spheres,
and in addition to that we have accomplished an enormous industrial development. How can you wonder
that we are political asses? There must be a weak
point somewhere."

Political sense connotes a sense of the general good.
That is just what the Germans lack. Politically
gifted nations, sometimes consciously, sometimes in-
stinctively, at the right moment, and even without
being driven by necessity, set the general interests of
the nation above their particular pursuits and desires.
It is a characteristic of the German to employ his
energy individually, and to subordinate the general
good to his narrower and more immediate interests.
That was what Goethe was thinking of in his cruel remark, so often quoted, that the Germans are very capable individually, and wretchedly inefficient in the bulk.

The instinct, proper to man, to unite in societies,
associations and communities for special purposes,
this natural, political instinct reaches its highest development in the community which forms a State.

Where this highest form of development is attained
consciously, the lower forms become of less and less
importance as a rule. Society, united for national
purposes, subordinates to itself all the smaller individual societies which serve ideal or material ends;
not forcibly or suddenly, but in the course of the
gradual expansion of national consciousness. The
progress of this development indicates the progress
of national unity and solidarity. Nations with a
strong political sense meet this development half
way, the German has often vigorously opposed it—
not on account of ill-will, or a lack of patriotic feeling, but following the dictates of his nature, which
feels more at home in small associations than when
included in the community of the whole nation.
Herr von Miquel once said to me in his caustic way,
as the result of forty years of parliamentary experience: "German Parliaments, in a comparatively
short space of time, mostly sink to the level of a district council, interested in nothing but local questions
and personal squabbles. In our Parliament a debate
rarely maintains a high level for more than one day;
on the second day the ebb begins, and then bagatelles
are discussed as futilely and in as much detail as possible." This inclination for individual and particular

things is responsible for the vogue for Associations and Clubs in Germany. The old joke that two Germans cannot meet without founding a club has a serious significance. The German feels at home in his clubs and societies. And if such an association exist for greater purposes of an industrial or a political kind, then its members, and especially its leaders, soon see in it the Archimedian point whence they would like to unhinge the whole political world. The late member of the Reichstag, von Kardorff, said to me, not long before his death: "Look, what maniacs we are about associations. The association itself becomes our be-all and end-all. The *Alliance Française* collected millions to establish French schools abroad, but it never dreamt of shaping the policy of the Government. Our Pan-German Association has done much to arouse national feeling, but, on the other hand, it considers itself the supreme court of appeal in questions of foreign policy. The Navy League has done great service in popularising the idea of a navy, but has not always resisted the temptation to prescribe to the Government and Reichstag what course to pursue in naval policy. The Association of Farmers, founded at a time of great stress in the agricultural world, has benefited the farmers as a whole very greatly, but has now reached such a point that it wants to treat everything in its own way, and runs great risk of overshooting the mark. We get so wrapped up in the idea of our association that we can see nothing beyond it."

In smaller things the German can easily find men of like ideas and like interests, but in great matters, very rarely. The more specialised the aim, the more quickly is a German association founded to further it; and, what is more, such associations are not temporary, but permanent. The wider the aim, the more slowly do the Germans unite to attain it, and the more liable they are, on the slightest excuse, to forsake this fellowship which cost so much trouble to found.

THE POLITICAL PAST OF THE GERMAN PEOPLE.

Our nation is undoubtedly, in a high degree, capable of uniting in strong and purposeful action in national movements. There are plenty of instances in our history. Thank Heaven, we have never entirely lacked national consciousness, enthusiasm, and self-sacrifice, and, in the times of greatest disruption, the feeling that all belonged to one nation never died out, but, on the contrary, grew to a passionate long-

ing.   Our periods of greatest political weakness,
times when the State was clearly in a state of collapse, were the most flourishing days of the intellectual life of our nation.   The classic writers of the
Middle Ages, as well as those of modern times, created our national literature in the midst of the decaying and decayed public life of the nation.

On the other hand, we, as a people, never lost the
consciousness of our political unity and independence
to such an extent as to bear the yoke of foreign rule
for any length of time.   In the hour of need the Germans found, in the depths of their hearts, the will and
the strength to overcome the national disintegration.
The War of Liberation a hundred years ago, which
has lesser prototypes in earlier centuries, will ever
remain a token of German national will-power and
love of liberty.

But in contradistinction to the nations that are,
politically speaking, more happily endowed, the expressions of German national unity are rather occasional than permanent.

> "I have sung of the Germans' June,
> But that will not last till October,"

was Goethe's lament not long after the War of Liberation.   Only too often with us the union dictated

by necessity was followed again by disruption into smaller political associations, states, tribes, classes; or, in modern times, into parties that preferred their own narrower tasks and aims to those of the nation at large, and degraded the great deeds of national unity by making them the object of ugly party quarrels.

In German history national unity is the exception, and separatism in various forms, adapted to the circumstances of the times, is the rule. This is true of the present as it was of the past.

Hardly any nation's history is so full of great successes and achievements in every sphere of man's activity. German military and intellectual exploits are unrivalled. But the history of no nation can tell of such an utter disproportion for centuries and centuries, between political progress on the one hand and capability and achievements on the other. The centuries of political impotence, during which Germany was crowded out of the ranks of the Great Powers, have little to tell of the defeat of German arms by foreign forces, with the exception of the time of Napoleon I. Our prolonged national misfortune was not due to foreigners; it was our own fault.

We first appear in history as a nation split up into

hostile tribes. The German Empire of mediæval times was not founded by the voluntary union of the tribes, but by the victory of one single tribe over the others, who for a long time unwillingly bore the rule of the stronger. The most brilliant period of our history, the period when the German Empire led Europe unopposed, was a time of national unity, in which the tribes and princes found a limit to their self-will in the will and the power of the Emperor. The Empire of the Middle Ages only succumbed in battle to the Papacy, because Roman politicians had succeeded in rousing opposition to the Emperor in Germany. The weakening of Imperial power afforded the princes a welcome opportunity for strengthening their own. While political life in Germany was split up into a large number of independent urban and territorial communities, in France, under the strong rule of her kings, a united State was formed, which took the place of Germany as leader of Europe.

Then came the religious split. The German territorial States, that for long had been united with the Empire in appearance only, became open enemies owing to the religious quarrel, and (a thing that is essentially characteristic of our nation) the German

States, Protestant as well as Catholic, did not hesitate to ally themselves with foreigners of a different persuasion, in order to fight fellow countrymen of a different persuasion. The religious wars set the German nation back centuries in its development; they almost destroyed the old Empire, except in name; they created the single independent States whose rivalry brought about struggles that filled the next two and a half centuries, until the foundation of the new German Empire. The Western and Northern Marches of Germany were lost and had to be recovered, in our times, at the point of the sword. The newly discovered world beyond the ocean was divided up among the other nations, and the German flag disappeared from the seas, and has only regained its rights within the last decades.

The ultimate national union was not achieved by peaceful settlement, but in the battle of German against German. And as the old Empire was founded by a superior tribe, so the new was founded by the strongest of the individual States. German history completed a circle, as it were. In a modern form, but in the old way, the German nation has, after a thousand years, once again, and more perfectly, completed the work which it accomplished in early times, and for whose destruction it alone was to blame.

Only a nation, sound to the core, and of indestructible vitality, could achieve this. True, we Germans have taken a thousand years to create, destroy and recreate, what for centuries other nations have possessed as the firm basis of their development—a national State. If we want to advance along the paths that the founding of our Empire has opened anew to us, we must insist on the suppression of such forces as might again endanger the unity of our national life. The best powers of Germany must not, as in olden times, be dissipated in struggles of the Imperial Government against individual States, and in struggles of the individual States against each other, without any consideration for the interests of the Empire.

THE GERMAN SEPARATIST SPIRIT IN THE NEW GERMAN EMPIRE.

The founding of the Empire overcame Germany's political disruption and changed our political life completely; but it was unable to change the character of the German people at the same time, or to transform our political shortcomings into virtues. The

German remained a separatist, even after 1871; different, and more modern, but still a separatist.

In the particularism of the single States, German separatism found its strongest but by no means its only possible expression. State separatism has impressed us most directly, because it was responsible, primarily, for the national disasters in German development during the last centuries. That is why all patriots wished to defeat it, and this desire was fulfilled by Bismarck. So far as man can tell, we need fear no serious injury to the unity of our national life from the special efforts of individual States. But we are none the less by no means free from manifestations of the separatist spirit. This spirit after, and even at the time of, the unification of Germany, sought a new field of political activity, and found it in the struggle of political parties.

The German party system, in contradistinction to that of other nations, which is in many cases older and more firmly rooted, possesses a specifically separatist character, and this is manifest in those points in which our party system differs from that of other countries. We have small parties that are sometimes formed for the sake of very narrow interests and objects, and carry on a struggle of their own which it is hardly possible to include in the affairs of a great Empire. The religious conflict in all its strength has found its way into our party system. The struggle between the various classes of society has retained almost all its vigour in the German party system, whereas in older civilised States the differences have been more and more completely adjusted by the industrial and social developments of modern times.

Our party system has inherited the dogmatism and small-mindedness, the moroseness and the spite that used to thrive in the squabbles of the German tribes and States. In other countries the party system is a national matter of home politics, and community of views with a foreigner is of no weight compared with the consciousness of belonging to the same nation as those of the opposite party at home. Abroad, the fact that the views of a political party are shared by foreigners is on occasion paraded in academic speeches at International Congresses, but it has little or no influence on practical politics. We Germans have strong movements in great parties, that demand the internationalisation of party ideas, and are not convinced that the party system has national limitations. Here again is a return in modern guise of an old German abuse. Among other nations it is self-understood that the special interests of a political party must be subordinated, not only to the greatest national interests, but also to any wider interest; it is in this point above all that our parties often fail. All too seldom in the German Empire do we comply with the emphatic command: "Country before party." Not so much because the German's love of his country is less than any foreigner's, but because his love of his party is so much greater. Consequently, a momentary success, or even a momentary manifestation of power by his own party, seems to the German so tremendously important—more important than the general progress of the nation.

It cannot be said that our German party struggles are carried on with more heat than in other countries. The German's political passion rarely rises to more than an average temperature, even in times of excitement, and that, at any rate, is a good thing. Amongst other nations, especially those of Latin race, the parties, in moments of stress, fling themselves at each other with an elemental passion that not seldom leads to excesses unknown to us Germans. But these heated outbursts, which are decisive for the success or defeat of a party or group of parties, are speedily followed there by overtures of peace and reconciliation. It is quite different here. We know nothing of the fanatic passion in excited conflicts which discharges itself like a thunder-cloud, but also, like a thunder-storm, clears the air of party politics. But we also lack the conciliatory spirit. If German parties have once opposed one another, even in matters of small political importance, it is only slowly and with difficulty that they forget and forgive each other. Occasional antagonism too often becomes lasting enmity, and, if possible, a fundamental difference in political principles is fabricated afterwards, though neither of the opposing parties was aware of it in the first instance. Very often, when discreet and well-meant attempts are made to bring about a reconciliation or agreement between parties holding strongly antagonistic convictions, this antagonism proves to have been discovered on the occasion of some quite recent party conflict, either about national questions of secondary importance, or even about a question of the power of a political party. Anyone who stands a little outside party machinery and the party rut often fails to understand why our parties cannot unite for the settlement of essentially unimportant questions of legislation, why they fight out slight differences of opinion on details of financial, social or industrial policy, with such acrimony as if the weal and woe of the Empire depended on them. No doubt praiseworthy German conscientiousness has some small part in this, but it is not the decisive factor. What is decisive is the fact that to each individual party the hatred of other parties seems of more essential importance than the legislative matter in question, which is often only seized as a welcome opportunity to emphasise the existing differences of party politics.

GERMAN PARTY SPIRIT AND PARTY LOYALTY.

Immutable loyalty within the party is the cause of their quarrelsomeness. Just because the German party man clings so steadfastly and even lovingly to his party, he is capable of such intense hatred of other parties and has such difficulty in forgetting insults and defeats suffered at their hands. Here again in modern guise we have the old German character. As the tribes and States were firmly knit together in themselves and quarrelled with each other, so the parties to-day. Proverbial German loyalty benefits the small political associations primarily, and the great national community only secondarily. A German Government will almost always sue in vain for the abundant loyalty which is spontaneously devoted to the party cause.   Even Bismarck experienced this. The man who got the better of the separatism of the States could not master the separatism of the parties. Although he had won the love and confidence of the German nation to a greater extent than anyone else, Prince Bismarck was seldom if ever successful in attempts to secure that devotion which was offered to party leaders.

Treitschke says somewhere that the hearts of the Germans have always belonged to poets and generals, not to politicians.   That is quite true, if we except the party leaders.   The Germans certainly forget them very soon after their death or retirement, but as long as their activity lasts they enjoy the whole-hearted loyalty and affection of all who belong to the party.   Ever since we have had political parties the popular men have been party men and party leaders, and their followers supported them even in opposition to Bismarck.   Right and wrong, success and failure, play an astonishingly small part in this. German loyalty to a party leader is self-sacrificing, unprejudiced and uncritical, as true loyalty which springs from love should be.   And it really makes no difference whether the party leader is successful

or not, whether he looks back on victories or defeats.
It has hardly ever happened in Germany that a party
refused to follow its leader, even if it was plain to
the meanest intelligence that he was taking them into
difficulties, let alone if it appeared that the tactics of
the party leaders were not in accordance with the
aims and objects of the State.

It has never been particularly difficult in Germany
to organise an opposition to the Government; but it
was always very hard to set up a movement of opposition within a party with any success. The hope
that the opposition party might fall to pieces at the
critical moment has nearly always proved deceptive.
After our party system had passed through the first
stage of ferment, which no young political system is
spared, and had become clarified by early changes and
modifications, the parties acquired remarkable solidarity. How often it has been foretold that a party
would split into so-called "modern" and "old" factions. Such forecasts have hardly ever been fulfilled.
Nowhere in our political life do we find such steadfast conservatism as in our parties. Even the radical
factions are thoroughly conservative as regards the
planks in their platform and their methods. This in-

ertia of party politics goes so far that the parties still cling to their old demands even when the general development of public affairs has rendered their fulfilment absolutely impossible.

The valiant loyalty of the German to his cause and his party leader is in itself beautiful and touching, morally deserving of respect as is all loyalty. Politics amongst us actually show a moral quality in this matter, whereas a well-known popular saying denies all possibility of morality in politics. But if we do discuss morality in politics, the question may well be raised whether, after all, there is not a higher form of political morality. All honour to loyalty in the service of the party, loyalty to principles and to leaders; but to serve one's country is better than to serve one's party. Parties do not exist for their own sakes, but for the common weal. The highest political morality is patriotism. A sacrifice of party convictions, disloyalty even to the party programme in the interest of the Empire, is more praiseworthy than party loyalty which disregards the general welfare of the country. Less party spirit and party loyalty, and more national feeling and more public spirit are what we Germans need.

PARTY INTERESTS AND NATIONAL INTERESTS.

Happily history proves that no party can permanently oppose national interests with impunity. Even the short history of German party politics furnishes instances. Liberalism, in spite of its change of attitude in national questions, has to this day not recovered from the catastrophic defeat which Prince Bismarck inflicted nearly half a century ago on the party of progress which still clung to the ideas and principles of 1848.

But epochs like that of 1866–1871, in which the soul of the nation was stirred to its depths, and judgment was pronounced so clearly and so pitilessly on political error, are as rare as they are great. The ordinary course of political development, as a rule, very slowly brings to light the results of mistaken party politics. Self-criticism and reflection must take the place of experience. It is easier for parties in other countries. In States where the parliamentary system obtains, parties are relieved of the difficult if noble task of educating themselves, the task imposed on our parties. In such countries a mistake in party politics is immediately followed by defeat and painful correction. I do not wish hereby to advocate the parliamentary system as it is understood in the west of Europe. The worth of a Constitution does not depend on the way it reacts on the party system. Constitutions do not exist for parties, but for the State. Considering the peculiarities of our Government, the parliamentary system would not be a suitable form of Constitution for us. Where this system proves of value, and that is by no means everywhere, the strength of the Government is based on the strength and value, on the political broad-mindedness and statesmanlike ability of the parties. There the parties formed the Constitution in the course of their own foundation and development as in England, as also in a certain sense in Republican France. In Germany the monarchical Governments are the supporters and creators of the Constitution. The parties are secondary formations, which could only grow in the soil of an existing State. We lack the preliminary conditions, both natural and historical, for a parliamentary system.

But the knowledge of this need not prevent us from seeing the advantages which this system gives to other States. Just as there is no absolutely perfect Constitution, so there is no absolutely defective one. The oft-repeated attempts, especially in France, to combine all the advantages of all possible Constitutions have hitherto always failed. While we realise this we need not shut our eyes to many advantages of Constitutions abroad.

In countries ruled by Parliament, the great parties and groups of parties acquire their political education by having to govern. When a party has gained a majority, and has provided the leading statesmen from its ranks, it has the opportunity of putting its political opinions into practice. If it pursues a theoretical or extreme course, if it sacrifices the common weal to party interests and party principles, if it has the folly to want to carry out its party programme undiluted and in full, it will lose its majority at the next elections and will be driven from office by the opposition. The party that must govern is responsible, not only for its own welfare, but in a higher degree for that of the nation and the State. Party interests and national interests coincide. But as it is not possible to govern a State for long in a one-sided fashion in accordance with some party programme, the party in office will moderate its demands in order not to lose its paramount influence over the country. The parties in a country governed by Parliament possess a salutary corrective that we lack, in the prospect of having to rule themselves, and the necessity of being able to do so.

In States not governed by Parliament the parties feel that their primary vocation is to criticise. They feel no obligation worth mentioning, to moderate their demands, or any great responsibility for the conduct of public affairs. As they never have to prove the practical value of their opinions *urbi et orbi,* they mostly content themselves with manifesting the immutability of their convictions. "A great deal of conviction, and very little feeling of responsibility." That is how a witty journalist once described our German party system to me, and he added: "Our parties do not feel as if they were the actors who perform in the play, but as if they were the critics who look on. They award praise and blame, but they do not feel as if they themselves participated in what goes on. The chief thing is to supply the voters at home with a strong and, if possible, welcome opinion."

Once, during the Boer War, standing in the lobby of the Reichstag, I remonstrated with one of the members on account of his attacks on England, which did not exactly tend to make our difficult position any easier. The worthy man replied in a tone of convic-

tion: "It is my right and my duty, as a member of
the Reichstag, to express the feelings of the German
nation. You, as Minister, will, I hope, take care
that my feelings do no mischief abroad." I do not
think that such a remark, the *naïveté* of which dis-
armed me, would have been possible in any other
country.

POLITICAL INTELLIGENCE AND POLITICAL FEELING.

There is nothing to be said against expressions of
feeling in politics, so long as they stop short of injuring the interests of the State. They belong to the
class of imponderables in political life, that men like
Bismarck valued highly. Particularly in Germany,
the feelings of the people have often acted as a whole-
some corrective to preconceived political opinions.
In foreign politics, feelings, sympathies and antipa-
thies are unreliable sign-posts, and we should not have
gone very far if our leading statesman had consulted
their hearts rather than their heads in shaping the
course of foreign relations.

In the field of home politics it is a different thing,
especially for us Germans. One is tempted to wish
that in that case political feelings and sentiments had
more than their actual influence, and political intelli-

gence less. For the effect of German political intelligence is not to moderate the desires of party
politics, nor to adapt their political demands to existing circumstances. Our political intelligence
urges us to systematise and schematise the realities
of political life; not to adjust things in a sensible way
to the existing political facts and conditions, but to
arrange these in a logically correct sequence of
thought.

We Germans are, on the one hand, a sentimental,
tender-hearted people, and are prone always, perhaps
too much so, to follow the dictates of our heart against
our better judgment. But, on the other hand, our
passion for logic amounts to fanaticism, and wherever
an intellectual formula or a system has been found for
anything, we insist with obstinate perseverance on
fitting realities into the system.

The individual German shows both these sides of
his nature in private life, the nation shows them in
public life, and many a curious phenomenon in the
present, as in the past, may be explained by this du-
ality of character. We like to consider foreign politics, which are connected with a long series of painful
and pleasurable national events, from the emotional
standpoint. Transactions in home politics, which the

nation grasped clearly in a comparatively short space of time, have become a recognised field for intellectual theories, for systematic examination and classification.

A German rarely applies the methods of modern science to politics, he mostly employs those of the old speculative philosophers. He does not attach importance to confronting Nature with open eyes and to observing what has happened, what is happening, and therefore what can and necessarily will happen again in the future. Rather, he grows intent upon finding out how things ought to have developed, and what they ought to have been like, for everything to harmonise with nice logic and for the system to come into its own. Their programmes are not adapted to reality; reality is to adjust itself to the programmes, and, what is more, not only in single instances, but altogether. Most of the German party programmes, if you consider them with an eye to their logic and systematic perfection, are extremely praiseworthy and redound to the credit of German thoroughness and logical conscientiousness. But, judged by the standard of practicability, not one will pass muster.

PARTY PLATFORMS.

Politics are life, and, like all life, will adhere to no rule. Modern politics are conditioned by events far back in our history, where the primary causes, whose effects we still feel, are lost in a mist of conjectures. But political practice would gain nothing by a complete knowledge of all causes and limitations. We should learn only how a multitude of things have come about, but not what must be done to-day or to-morrow. Nearly every day brings new facts and new problems which require new decisions, just as in the lives of individual men. Nor does the labour demanded by the day and by the hour see the end of our task. We must, as far as lies in the power of our understanding and ability, take thought for the future. Of what assistance, then, are the regulations of a programme drawn up at a certain moment, however uniform and logical it be?

The varied life of a nation, ever changing, ever growing more complicated, cannot be stretched or squeezed to fit a programme or a political principle. Of course, the parties must draw up in the form of a programme the demands and ideas they represent, so as to make it clear to the country, especially at election time, what are their aims and principles. Without a programme, a party would be an unknown quantity. But when a programme, drawn up to serve the immediate and future aims of party politics, is petrified into a system for all politics in general, it becomes objectionable. There are many and often conflicting interests among the people, and the representatives of like interests are quite right to band themselves together and formulate their demands. The formula is the programme. There are different opinions about State, Law and Society, about the regulation of public life, especially in respect of the distribution of political rights between the people and the Government. Those, also, who represent similar views will join together and express their opinions in a few distinctive propositions. These propositions constitute the programme. The connection between industrial life and political life often causes the representatives of like interests to hold like political opinions. Their programme will be proportionately more comprehensive. It may also be admitted that the two concrete, historical views of State and Society—the Conservative and the Liberal—and the two abstract, dogmatic views—the Ultramontane and the Social-Democratic—embrace a large number of the facts of political life. The respective party programmes can therefore go into detail accordingly. But here, too, there is a limit. A large number of events in public life cannot be included even in these comparatively comprehensive programmes, nor can Conservatives and Liberals hold different views with respect to them. On the whole, there is a preponderance of such legislative problems as deal with questions of pure utility, which must be solved by political common sense, and cannot be weighed in the scales of general party views. But such disregard of party programmes is rarely conceded, even to the details of legislation. It does not suffice us Germans to confine our party politics to a certain number of practical demands and political opinions. Each party would like to imbue politics as a whole with its views, even down to the smallest detail. And this is not limited to politics. The parties would like to be distinguished from one another even in their grasp of intellectual and their conception of practical life. Party views are to become a "Weltanschauung" (Conception of the Universe). Herein they over-estimate political and under-estimate intellectual life. The German nation in particular has been more deeply and seriously moved by the great problems of a conception of the Universe than any other nation. It has often, probably too often for its particular interests, subordinated dry questions of policy to the battle about the conception of the Universe. On the other hand, it was the first nation to set intellectual life free from political tutelage. If now it subordinates this conception to party politics, if it wants to go so far as to see every event in the world and in life, in the dismal light of political party principles, it will be false to itself. The attempt to widen the scope of politics, and especially party politics, in this way must lead to an intellectual decline, and has perhaps already done so. A political conception of the Universe is nonsense, for luckily the world is not everywhere political. And a conception of the Universe founded on party politics cannot even span the political world, because there are far too many matters and questions in politics that lie outside the sphere of party platforms and party principles.

An English friend once said to me that it struck him how often the words, "Conception of the Universe," occurred in the German parliamentary speeches. Over and over again he found, "From the point of view of my conception of the Universe, I cannot approve of this, and I must demand that." He let me explain to him what German party politicians meant by "Conception of the Universe," and then remarked, as he shook his head, that English politicians and members of Parliament did not know much about such things. They had different opinions and represented different interests, pursued different objects; but they only argued on practical grounds and rarely touched on such high matters as the conception of the Universe. We Germans really are not differentiated from the matter-of-fact Englishmen on this point, by greater depth and thoroughness, but by a mistaken estimate of political ideas. When we try to make of party principles a system by which to judge all political and non-political life, we harm ourselves politically and intellectually. Politically, we only intensify the differences which in any case we feel particularly keenly, because we attribute a special intellectual value to them, and we reduce more and more the number of those tasks in public life which really can be carried out much better without the bias of party politics. But if we drag questions of intellectual life into the realm of party politics, that will mean the loss of that intellectual versatility and magnanimity which have won for German culture the first place in the civilised world.

In Germany a politician or a statesman is very quickly reproached with lack of principle if, under pressure of shifting conditions, he changes an opinion he used to hold, or approves of the views of more than one party. But development takes place without reference to party platforms or principles. If forced to choose between sacrificing an opinion and doing a foolish thing, the practical man will prefer the former alternative. At any rate, no Minister, who is responsible to the nation for his decisions, can afford to indulge in the luxury of a preconceived opinion, when it is a question of fulfilling a legitimate demand of the times. And if, then, it is pointed out that there is a contradiction between his present view and his earlier expressions of opinion, I can only advise him to protect himself against the reproach of being inconsistent, a turncoat, a weathercock, and whatever the other catchwords of vulgar polemics may be, by acquiring a thick skin, which is in any case a useful thing to have in modern public life. It is a fact confirmed by all experience that the true interests of the nation have never been found in the course of one particular party alone. They always lie midway between the courses pursued by various parties. We must draw the diagonal of the parallelogram of forces.

It will sometimes tend more in the direction of one party and sometimes in that of another. A Minister, whatever party he may incline to personally, must try to find a compromise between all the legitimate demands made by the various parties. In the course of a fairly long term of office little by little, and as his tasks vary, he will, of course, be attacked by all parties. But that does not matter so long as the country prospers. I never took the reproach of lack of political principle tragically; I have even, at times, felt it to savour of praise, for I saw in it appreciation of the fact that I was guided by reasons of State. The political principles which a Minister has to live up to are very different in character from the principles recognised by a party man; they belong to the sphere of State policy, not of party politics. A Minister must be loyal to the general interests of the State and of the people which are entrusted to his care, and this without considering party platforms, and, if necessary, in opposition to all parties, even to that with which the majority of his political views are in accordance. In a Minister, firm principles and impartiality are not only compatible, they are interdependent. Bismarck was a man of iron principles, and by being true to them he led our country to unity, glory and greatness. As a Member of Parliament he was a party man, and as Minister he was reproached by his party for a political change of front. He was accused ten years later of again changing his opinions. As a matter of fact, he never swerved from the path which led to his goal, for his goal was nothing less than to secure prosperity and every possible advantage for the German nation and the Empire. This goal could not be attained on party lines, for the interests of the community in general seldom, if ever, coincide with those of a single party.

Universally applicable rules for the best possible policy cannot well be drawn up. Political ends and political means vary with circumstances, and one must not slavishly imitate any model, not even the greatest. In as far as varied and chequered life can be summed up in a formula, for politics it would run as follows: Fanatical where the welfare and interests of the country and where reasons of State are in question, idealistic in aim, realistic in political practice, sceptical, as far as men, their trustworthiness and gratitude are concerned.

II

NATIONAL VIEWS AND THE PARTIES

I HAVE never concealed the fact, even from Liberals, that in many great questions of politics I share the views of the Conservatives. In the same way I have never denied the fact that I am not a Conservative party man. As a responsible Minister I could not be that, given the character of my office and our German conditions. I discuss here what my personal reasons are for not being a party man, although I consider myself a Conservative in all essentials, because the consideration of these reasons leads to concrete questions of German politics at the present time and in the immediate past.

CONSERVATISM.

There is a distinct difference between State Conservatism that the Government can pursue and party Conservatism that no Government in Germany can adhere to without falling into a state of partisanship which, in all circumstances, must prove fatal. In other words: The policy of the Government can go

hand in hand with the policy of the Conservatives, so
long as the latter is in accordance with the true interests of the State. That was, and is, not seldom the
case. But the ways of the Government and the Conservatives must diverge, if the policy of the party is
not in accordance with the interests of the community
which the Government must protect. At the same
time, the Government can be more conservative towards the party than the party towards the Government. More conservative in the sense that it fulfils
more perfectly the special task of upholding the State.
In such situations Prince Bismarck, too, who was a
Conservative consciously and by conviction, came
into bitter conflict with his former party friends. It
is well known that he dealt in detail with this very
point, both in his "Gedanken and Erinnerungen"
("Thoughts and Recollections") and in the conversa-
tions which Poschinger has transmitted to us.

The task of Conservative policy was once aptly
defined by Count Posadowsky in the following way:
That Conservatives must maintain the State in such
a way that the people are content in it. Such a maintenance of the State is often unimaginable without the
alteration of existing institutions. The State must
adjust itself to modern conditions of life, in order

to remain habitable and consequently vigorous.

It would be very unjust to deny that the Conservative party has often assisted in introducing innovations; sometimes, indeed, with a better grace than those parties which have "Progress" inscribed on their banner. This was the case in the year 1878, when industrial conditions necessitated the great revolution in tariffs and industrial policy. Again, at the inauguration of the social policy which took into account the changed conditions of the labouring classes. But at times the interests represented by the Conservative party were opposed to the interests which the Government defended, in order to preserve the community's satisfaction in the State. Owing to the intensification of economic differences, the Conservative party, like all others, has, in a certain sense, come to represent special interests. I will not discuss the point whether this is the case to such an extent as to be bad for the party. But no one who has sat on the Front Bench during the last decades will be prepared to deny that it is true to a greater extent than is favourable to the course of the Government's affairs.

I had to withdraw further from the Conservative party in proportion as it represented certain interests, and I could not reconcile these with those of the community. In the fight over the Tariff the interests of the nation in general were identical with those of the Conservative party; but in the reform of the Imperial finances they were not. The subsequent development in both cases proved this to be true. Nothing in the fundamental views of the Conservative party in respect of the organisation of society, industries and, above all, of the State ever separated me from it, nor does it do so to-day.

THE CONSERVATIVE ELEMENT IN PRUSSO-GERMAN HISTORY.

We must never fail to appreciate what the Conservative element has achieved for the political life of Prussia and Germany. It would be a sad loss to the nation if Conservative views ceased to be a living and effective force among the Germans, and if the party ceased to occupy a position in parliamentary and political life which is worthy of its past. The forces which animate the Conservative party are those which made Germany great, and which our country must preserve in order to remain great and grow greater; they are forces which never become out of date. We Germans must not lose the ideals of the best Conservatism; manly loyalty without servility to the King and the reigning family, and tenacious attachment to home and country.

If, nowadays, the opponents of the Conservative party are not content to fight them on the ground of party differences, but manifest class-hatred, always so objectionable in political life, against those classes of the nation which are chiefly represented in the Conservative party, we must not forget what those very classes did in the service of Prussia and Germany. It was the noblemen and peasants east of the Elbe who, under the Hohenzollern princes, primarily achieved greatness for Brandenburg and Prussia. The throne of the Prussian Kings is cemented with the blood of the Prussian nobility. The Great King (Frederick the Great) expressed emphatically more than once how well his nobles had served him.

The praise which the Prussian nobility demand, and which they have a perfect right to expect, is not meant to detract from the achievements and merits of other classes. Without the self-sacrificing loyalty of the middle classes, the peasants and the poor people, the nobility would have accomplished little. It is quite true, too, that the nobles were able to distinguish themselves particularly in earlier times, because the conditions at that period gave them exceptional opportunities. But it was when they occupied posts of responsibility and danger in the service of the Prussian State that they achieved most—more than the aristocracy of any other modern State. Nothing but injustice can fail to recognise this.

It is altogether preposterous, nowadays, still to contrast the nobility and the bourgeoisie as separate castes. Professional and social life have so fused the old classes that they can no longer be distinguished from each other.

But if one appreciates at its true value the efficiency of the old classes in the past, one must be just and concede the merits of each. The Prussian nobles have a right to be proud of their past. If they keep the sentiments of their ancestors alive in the ideals of the Conservative party, they deserve thanks for so doing. And it must not be forgotten that such old Prussian sentiments guided the policy of the Conservative party in the most difficult times of our old Emperor and his great Minister, in the years of conflict. So far as one can speak of a right to gratitude in politics—and one ought to be able to do so—we owe the Conservatives a debt of gratitude for the support they afforded Bismarck in the year 1862. I lay particular stress on this, because at the time my official career was nearing its close I was forced to oppose the Conservative party, and because I am absolutely convinced that the Conservative faction went astray in the year 1909. I should like to make a clear distinction between my general attitude towards Conservative views, my sentiments towards the Conservative party, and my opinion of individual phases of Conservative party politics.

Even a man who esteems the fundamental views of the Conservatives as highly as I do, who, like me, hopes that sound Conservative thought will have a far-reaching influence on legislation, and who has often furthered such influence, must be of opinion that disastrous consequences will result from the fact that in 1909 the bridges between the Right and Left were broken down. The really fruitful periods of our home policy were those when the Right and the Left co-operated. In saying this I refer, not only to the time of the so-called "Block Policy," but also to earlier, well-known and significant phases of Bismarck's time.

CONSERVATISM AND LIBERALISM.

Conservatism and Liberalism are not only both justified, but are both necessary for our political life.

How difficult it is to rule in our country is made clear by the facts that one cannot rule in Prussia for any length of time without the support of the Conservatives, nor in the Empire without that of the Liberals. Neither must Liberal ideas disappear from us as a people. Moreover, the formation of strong Liberal parties is indispensable to us. If Conservatism is rooted in the administrative talent of the old Prussians, Liberalism is rooted in the intellectual peculiarities of the German nation. Its best ideals, too, are of permanent value. We Germans do not want to be deprived of the lusty defence of individual freedom against State coercion, and this Liberalism has always represented.

Liberalism, too, has earned its historic rights and its right to gratitude. It was the Liberals who first expressed the idea of German Unity, and spread it through the people. They carried out the indispensable preliminary work. The goal could not be reached by the course which they followed. Then Conservative policy had to step in, in order, as Bismarck expressed it, to realise the Liberal idea by means of a Conservative action. The German Empire itself may well be regarded as the first, the greatest, and the most successful piece of work accomplished by the co-operation of the Conservatives and Liberals.

It is at present customary in both camps to look upon Conservatism and Liberalism as two fundamentally opposed conceptions of the State, and to assert that each lives on its antagonism to the other. That does not, however, correctly interpret the relationship between German Conservatives and Liberals. If it were true, the two parties, and the groups which are attached to them, would have to gain in strength the stronger became the contrast between them, and the more hostile the attitude they adopted towards each other.

But the exact opposite is the case. With the exception of a few extraordinary situations, the Conservatives and Liberals have been strongest as parties and most influential in Parliament when they co-operated. The two parties were strongest in the Cartel and in the Block. And the periods of their co-operation were always those when the temper of the nation as a whole was most cheerful and hopeful.

No doubt we must not expect all political salvation, or the solution of all legislative problems, to result from co-operation between Conservatives and Liberals. It will happen again and again that their ways part as regards individual, and also important, questions. For the antagonism exists, and rightly so. It would also be quite wrong to credit the co-operation of Conservatives and Liberals with all great achievements in the sphere of home politics. The Centre played a distinguished and often a decisive part in our social legislation, in many of our Armament Bills, and, above all, in granting us the Navy. But strife between the Conservatives and the Liberals has always been disastrous—for the two parties themselves, for the course of our home policy, and, last but not least, for the temper of the nation.

The antagonism between Liberals and Conservatives will never disappear. It has an historical and a practical significance. This friction is a part of our political life. But the antagonism in their views should not be exaggerated unnecessarily, nor made to involve such great matters as utterly irreconcilable conceptions of the Universe. In so doing one departs from sober political reality. Even religious antagonism which has been amongst us for four centuries, and which the nation, in accordance with its disposition, has always taken very seriously, makes way for the demands of the moment. In Socialism we really have a series of ideas, so different from our homely conceptions of Law and Custom, Religion, Society and State that it may indeed be termed a different conception of the Universe. I myself, in this connection, once spoke of a difference in the conception of the Universe. But that a middle-class Liberal differs from a middle-class Conservative in his conception of the Universe no one seriously believes. They have too many common ideas and ideals, especially in national matters, and the wide kingdom of German intellectual life in Science and in Art belongs to them both. How many Liberals there are who incline to individual Conservative views! How many Conservatives who are by no means opposed to all Liberal ideas and demands! All these people do not consider themselves politically neutral, nor are they. And what about the Ministers? The party papers quarrel at regular intervals whether this Minister or that other is to be stamped as a Conservative or as a Liberal, and as a rule each party tries to foist the majority of Ministers on to the opposing party. The fact is that, if asked to state precisely to which party platform they give their support, most Ministers would be at a loss.

It is not only unjustifiable, but also unpractical, to emphasise unduly the differences between the parties.

They do not, as a rule, go hand in hand for any length of time, and the bonds that unite them are anything but permanent. So if they break with their friends of yesterday, and become reconciled to their enemies of yesterday, they are placed in the awkward position of having to break down the carefully constructed fabric of fundamental party differences, with as much trouble as they expended in building it up. This has happened just about as often as the composition of the majority changed.

If party differences really went so deep, and permeated so completely every detail of political life as is represented in party quarrels, then, considering the number of our parties, none of which has hitherto obtained an absolute majority, it would be impossible to accomplish any legislative work.

But, as a matter of fact, much valuable work of different kinds has been done in almost every department of home politics during the last decades. One after the other, the parties have placed themselves at each other's disposal, and have often, with astounding suddenness, overcome the differences they emphasised so strongly before. No doubt other differences are emphasised all the more strongly. And it only lasts until the formation of a new majority, so that really there is no occasion to take the antagonism between the parties so tragically.

THE GOVERNMENT AND THE PARTIES.

The Government must also look upon party antagonism as a variable quantity. Not only as a quantity variable in itself, but as one whose variability can and must be influenced if the interests of the Empire and the State demand it. It is not sufficient to take majorities wherever they are to be found and as occasion offers. The Government must try to create majorities for its tasks.

To govern with a majority which varies in each case is no doubt advantageous and convenient, but there are great dangers attached to it. It is certainly not a panacea for all political situations.

Bismarck is usually cited as having taken his majorities where he could get them. But in this, as in most references to the time of Bismarck, the point is missing—Bismarck himself at the head of the Government. He held the reins of Government with such an iron grip that he never ran any risk of letting the least scrap of power slip into the hands of Parliament through the influence he conceded to a majority, when he happened to find one at his disposal. Above all, he never dreamt of considering the wishes of a majority unless they tallied with his own. He made use of existing majorities, but he never let them make use of him. Bismarck in particular excelled in ridding himself of antagonistic majorities and in procuring such as would acquiesce in the aims of his policy. If his choice lay between allowing an important law to be blocked or mangled by an existing majority and engaging in a troublesome fight to effect a change of majority, he never hesitated to choose the latter. He profited by the possibility of getting casual majorities, but he was the last to yield to such.

In this respect Bismarck's name should not be idly cited. His rule can only serve as a precedent for a strong, determined and even ruthless Government, not for an accommodating and yielding one that concedes greater rights to the parties than they are entitled to claim.

It is certainly less trouble to look on and see how a majority can be got together for a Bill, than to see that the Bill is passed in the way the Government thinks proper and profitable.

If the Government allows itself to be led, then it may easily happen that, what with the feuds of the parties and the haggling between the sections which

make up the majority, the Bill will become unrecog-
nisable and something quite different will result—at
times even just the contrary to what the Government
wanted. In this way the majorities are not put at
the disposal of the Bills that the Government intro-
duces as opportunity affords, but the Government
give their Bills up to the majorities to pass and
amend as they see best. While the Government pre-
tends to be above the parties, in reality it slips under
their heel.

The very necessity for changing the majorities, in
view of the state of the parties in Germany, demands
a strong hand to direct the affairs of the Government. No Government can work for ever with one
and the same majority. That is rendered impossible
by the relations which the parties bear to one another, by the dogmatism of most parties, by their
tendency to go over to the opposition from time
to time in order to gain popularity, and, finally,
by the manifold nature of the Government's tasks,
which can only in part be accomplished by one
particular majority. In the interests of a policy
which as far as possible does justice to all sections of the nation, it is not desirable that any one
of the parties, with whose assistance positive work

for the good of the State can be done, should never co-operate. It is good for the parties if they have a share in legislative work. Parties which always preserve an attitude of opposition and negation, and are left alone by the Government, grow pedantic in the items of their programmes, and, if they do not die out altogether, at best deprive our public life of valuable forces. In the course of the last decades the Left Wing of our Liberalism had fallen into this condition, even with regard to vital questions of national importance. The problem of enrolling Ultra-Liberalism in the forces useful to the nation had to be tackled. It was solved by the "Block Policy," and this solution not only proved satisfactory during the existence of the Block, but still works at the present time, for the Ultra-Liberals helped to procure a very substantial increase in the army.

THE BLOCK.

The formation of the group of parties which goes by the somewhat unfortunate name of the "Block," a term borrowed from French politicians, was an event of extraordinary and typical significance, and was most enlightening. If only because I do not like to prophesy, I will not attempt any exhaustive discussion as to whether the era of the Block was merely an episode. It can hardly be denied that events may at any time bring about a similar situation, if not the same. But this does not convey that I recommend the Block as a panacea for any and every contingency in home politics. I was always well aware that such a combination must be of limited duration, because, for one thing, it never entered my calculations that the Centre would permanently be excluded. But it seems to me that this period, short as it was, sheds a special light on the most important problems of our home politics. In my opinion, and that of the majority of my countrymen, these most important problems are: National questions, and the fight against the Social Democrats. Of course there are many other problems in addition, by the solving of which we do nothing towards the solution of the great problems. A deep scrutiny and proper understanding of our home policy shows that it is ultimately dominated by these two great questions.

A distinction must be made between the immediate occasion and the indirect causes which led to the combination of 1907. The events which necessitated the dissolution of the Reichstag in 1906 are still present to the minds of all. Owing to the attitude of the Centre, an untenable situation had been created, and it was desirable for the Government to take action which would have more than a transitory effect. The attempts of the Centre to interfere in colonial administration had reached such a pitch that, merely in the interests of discipline, they could be tolerated no longer. The requisitions for the troops in South-West Africa, who were heroically fighting a cruel enemy amidst great hardships, were rejected by the Centre and the Social Democrats; and, finally, there was an attempt to interfere with the power of chief command possessed by the Emperor. Principles of State were at stake which could not be sacrificed. A Government which in such case does not resort even to extreme measures of protection is not worthy of the name. I never for a moment failed to realise what inconvenience was entailed by dissolving the Reichstag, and thus breaking with a party so powerful and tenacious as the Centre. My political life would have been much pleasanter if I had consented to some sort of a compromise, however unsatisfactory. But this was one of those moments which in the interests of the country demand battle. A Government that at such a period hesitates to plunge into the fray for fear of subsequent difficulties, consults its own interest before the country's. In this case the military principle holds good that attack is preferable to defence. The Government exists for the good of the country, not the country for the Government. I had warned the Centre in good time of the consequences of their behaviour. If afterwards it was asserted that the Centre did not realise what the final upshot would be, I can point to my speeches in the Reichstag and my declarations in those anxious days, which more than refute these statements.

If, after speeches such as I made on November 28 and December 4, 1906, I had not either dissolved the Reichstag or handed in my resignation, I should not have dared to show myself in public. When the majority, consisting of the Centre, the Social Democrats, Poles and Alsatians, insisted on reducing the supplementary estimates for South-West Africa from 29 to 20 million (marks), and also demanded a decrease in the colonial force in that part of the country where the rising had only just been put down, the Reichstag was dissolved. The important thing then was to win a majority at the elections for the Conservatives and Liberals of all shades who had supported the Government.

The attitude of the Centre and the Social Democrats in regard to colonial policy, and, above all, the attempt to tamper with the Emperor's prerogative by virtue of his power as chief in command, accorded by the Constitution, to decide the strength of the troops required at the time by the military situation in South-West Africa, were sufficient reason to necessitate a change in the composition of the majority by means of a General Election. But, apart from these immediate causes, it seemed to me, and to an overwhelming number of patriotic Germans as well, that a change in the grouping of the parties and in their relative strength was eminently desirable.

It has been said that in 1907 we started a campaign against the Centre, and by chance beat the Social Democrats. That, of course, is a misinterpretation of the facts. If a Government brings about a General Election, it is not a question of a punitive expedition against one particular party; but it is because the Government wants to make a change in the composition of the majority. The Cartel elections of 1887 followed the same course as the Block elections twenty years later. The Centre emerged from both unharmed. But both fulfilled their object by shattering the other parties which at the time united with the Centre in forming the opposition. In the first case it was the Ultra-Liberals, later it was the Social

Democrats. War was declared on the oppositional majority as such. Compared with this primary object, the question as to which party should be weakened in order to decimate the majority was of secondary importance. At the Block elections I preferred a weakening of the Social Democrats to a corresponding loss of seats on the part of the Centre. At that time, and, what is more, entirely on my own initiative, at the second ballots I passed the word for the Centre against the Social Democrats. It was at my express request that the former burgomaster of Cologne, His Excellency Herr Becker, invited support for the Centre against the Social Democrats. Since then I have often been told that this was a mistake, and that I myself had assisted in creating a majority of Conservatives and the Centre, which made it very difficult for me to govern later on. To this very day I am of opinion that I did quite right at the time. On the one hand, I had no intention of permanently excluding the Centre; on the other, there was never any question of my being supported by the Social Democrats.

THE CENTRE.

The Centre is the strong bastion built by the Roman Catholic section of the people to protect itself from interference on the part of the Protestant majority. The previous history of the Centre may be traced back to the times when in the old Empire the *Corpus Evangelicorum* was opposed by the *Corpus Catholicorum.* But whereas in the old Empire Catholicism and Protestantism were more or less evenly balanced, in the new Empire the Catholics are in the minority; the old Catholic Empire has been succeeded by the new Protestant one.

It must, however, be admitted that the Catholic minority has a great advantage over the Protestant majority in its unity and solidarity. Good Protestant as I am, I do not deny that, though the Protestants often have reason to complain of lack of perception on the part of the Catholics, yet, on the other hand, in Protestant circles there is often a lack of toleration towards the Catholics. Members of both religions would do well to take to heart the beautiful words of Görres: "All of us, Catholics and Protestants, have sinned in our fathers, and still weave the tissue of human error in one way or another. No one has the right to set himself above another in his pride, and God will tolerate it in none, least of all in those who call themselves His friends." My old Commander, later General Field-Marshal

Freiherr von Loë, a good Prussian and a good Catholic, once said to me that in this respect matters would not improve until the well-known principle of French law, "que la recherche de la paternité était interdite," were changed for us into "la recherche de la confession était interdite." He also replied to this effect to a Royal lady from abroad, who asked what was the percentage of Protestant and Catholic officers in his army corps: "I know how many battalions, squadrons and batteries I command, but I take no interest in what church my officers belong to." That is what they think in the army, and in the Diplomatic Corps, and this manner of thinking must hold in other positions as well. The feeling of being slighted, which still obtains in many Catholic circles, can only be overcome by an absolutely undenominational policy, a policy in which, as I once expressed it in the Chamber of Deputies, there is neither a Protestant nor a Catholic Germany, but only the one indivisible nation, indivisible in material as in spiritual matters.

On the other hand, however, there are many weighty reasons why a religious party should not wield such an extraordinary and decisive influence in politics as was the case for many years in this country. The Centre is, and will remain, a party held together by religious views, however subtly opinion in Cologne and Berlin may argue about the idea of a religious party. The Centre is the representative of the religious minority. As such its existence is justified; but it must not arrogate to itself a predominant position in politics. Doubtless every party which, owing to the constitution of the majority and to its own strength, occupies an exceptionally strong position in Parliament, is inclined to abuse its power. The Ultra-Liberals did so in the years of struggle; the National Liberals in the first half of the 'seventies; the Conservatives in the Prussian Chamber of Deputies, when they thwarted the well-thought-out and far-reaching plans for the canal; and finally the Centre did so. All my predecessors in office were in such a position as to have to ward off the Centre's claims to power. Many of the conflicts in home politics during the last decades had their origin in the necessity the Governments were under to defend themselves; the conflict of 1887, that of 1893, and, finally, the battle of 1906.

For a party which is in an almost impregnable position, such as the Centre occupies, the temptation to pursue a policy of power pure and simple is very great. It is doubly tempting if the Centre is in a po-

sition to form a majority together with the Social
Democrats, and with their help can prevent the passing of any and every Bill. A majority composed of
the Centre and the Social Democrats, that resists national demands, is not only injurious to our national
life, but constitutes a serious danger.

Before 1906 the Centre allowed itself to be tempted
to turn to its own advantage the systematic opposition of the Social Democrats towards national requisitions, if together with these it could obtain a majority, and if it fitted in with its policy of power
to discomfit the Government by the rejection of
such requisitions. In the same way, before the storm
which cleared the air in 1906, it happened more than
once that the Centre laid down difficult or even impossible conditions, before giving its consent to national
requisitions, knowing full well that without its help
it was impossible to get a national majority. From
the defeat of the Cartel at the February elections of
1890 up to the Block elections of 1907, after which the
Centre did not oppose any Army, Navy or Colonial
Bills, the Government lived uninterruptedly under
the shadow of a threat of union between the Centre
and the Social Democrats, to form a majority for the
Opposition. In the seventeen years between the Car-

tel and the Block, the Centre certainly rendered valuable services in furthering national affairs, especially
in respect of the Navy Bills, the Tariff Bills, and in a
notable manner in the development of social policy.
But events in the sphere of colonial politics in the
winter of 1906 proved that the Centre still regarded
the rejection of national requisitions, with the aid of
the Social Democrats, as a welcome and legitimate
means of carrying out its policy of power.

THE TASK OF 1907.

It was necessary to settle the conflict conjured up
by the Centre together with the Social Democrats. the
Poles and the Alsatians, not only for the time being,
but with an eye to the past and the future.   The need
of forming a majority for national questions without
the Centre had really existed since the split in the Bis-
marckian Cartel, and was created by the conclusions
that the Centre had drawn from the fact that its assistance was indispensable for the furtherance of national affairs.   So it was an old problem that was set
for solution in 1907, one that was made urgent by the
divisions of the preceding months, but that was not
originally raised by them: a national majority without the Centre.   Not a majority against the Centre,

nor a national majority from which the Centre was to be excluded, but a national majority, powerful and strong enough in itself to do justice to national exigencies, if need be without the help of the Centre. If this were achieved the Centre could no more harbour the seductive idea that it was indispensable, and the danger of a majority formed by the Centre and the Social Democrats would no longer be acute. When the People's party voted with the Conservatives and National Liberals for the Colonial Bills, I perceived the possibility of forming a new national majority. I should have seized this opportunity, even if I had not been convinced that it was possible to smooth away the differences between the Conservatives and Liberals, and that the co-operation of these two parties would have great educative value. In pursuing this course I did my duty. The Block majority was formed not against the Centre as such, but against the Centre, allied in opposition, with the Social Democrats. The nation looked upon the Block elections as a purely national matter. The temper of the people, when success was assured, was not such as would be roused by a triumph in party politics, but as would emanate from a feeling of patriotic satisfaction. The Block had been matured by the experience of nearly two decades of home policy. There was promise for the coming decade in the fact that the last of the middle-class parties had been won over in support of the national tasks of the Empire.

The underlying idea of the so-called Block was similar to that which was at the foundation of the Cartel. I might almost say: the Block was the modern realisation of an old idea adapted to the changed circumstances of the times. For a long time it had not been feasible to repeat the Cartel formed by Conservatives and National Liberals. The old parties of the Cartel had been ground so small between the millstones of the Centre and the Social Democrats that there was no longer hope of renewing the Cartel majority for some time to come. In order to be able, if need be, to dispense with the help of the Centre in forming a national majority, it was necessary to include Ultra-Liberalism. When in 1906 the Ultra-Liberals offered to co-operate in national work, the Government had to seize the helping hand held out to them—and hold it fast. It was not so much a question of winning over a party to the Government side, as of extending the sphere of the national idea among the people. For the first time since the founding of the Empire, the old Ultra-Liberalism wheeled into the front rank of the nation. The way in which this was done hardly left a doubt that the change was intended to be permanent rather than temporary. What Eugen Richter had prophesied to me, not long before he retired from political life, had come true. With sure instinct, all classes of the nation felt and understood the real significance of this turn of affairs in 1906, till later on the fads of party programmes obscured the clear facts, as they have so often done.

The years of the Block brought great success and taught an important lesson. The national vanguard was widened, and it was proved that the Social Democrats can be repulsed: both points of significant gain in the solution of the most important problems of our home policy.

Since 1907 the Ultra-Liberals have been ranged on the side of the National party. The small Army and Navy Bills of the spring of 1912 were accepted by them in the same way as were the great increase in the Army in the summer of 1913, and the demands of colonial policy. To estimate the value of the assistance of the Ultra-Liberals, it is not sufficient to consider whether the Armament Bills would have had a majority in the Reichstag without them. The advantage lies in this, that whereas formerly a majority of middle-class parties stood security for the national needs of the Empire, a majority which was mostly got together with great difficulty, now all the middle-class parties stand united against the Social Democrats and the Nationalistic parties and fragments of parties. The national questions of the Empire have ceased to be a subject of anxiety in home politics. And the solid force with which the national idea finds expression in all sections of the middle classes, when the defence of the Empire is concerned, must be set down as a valuable asset for the prestige of Germany abroad.

CONCERNING THE HISTORY OF THE GERMAN POLICY OF ARMAMENTS.

In order to measure the progress made, it is only necessary to consider the fate of the bigger Armament Bills during the last decades. This is all the more significant as the national idea must act, not only in the direction of the Continental policy of Prussia and Germany so glorious in the past, but also in the direction of the new world policy, whose importance in the meantime lies more in the future. Not only the army, but also the navy, is concerned to-day. The middle-class parties in the Reichstag have to advocate considerable material sacrifices in the country for disbursements for national purposes, and they must therefore lay greater stress on the national idea.

It is certainly a curious fact that in the most military and most warlike of the European nations the parties have resigned themselves so unwillingly to new demands for the defence of the Empire that it has taken more than three and a half decades to achieve unanimity, at least among the middle-class parties. The blame for this attitude attaches, not so much to lack of patriotism, as to that desire for power in party politics, and that obstinate devotion to the party programme, to which I have earlier referred. It was the task of the Government to waken the latent patriotic feelings of all middle-class parties, to animate them, and spontaneously, and without prejudice, to uphold them when they seemed strong enough to co-operate in a practical manner in the work of the Empire. A German Government would act against the welfare of the nation if, owing to party prejudices of its own, it should repulse the national zeal of a party, and if the sacrifices of a party in the interests of the nation should seem of less value because its general trend in politics did not fall in with the Government's ideas. For the Government the intensity of national feeling is by far the most important quality of a party.

It will and must be possible to work with a party that is at bottom reliable from the national standpoint, for such a party will ultimately allow itself to be influenced in favour of national interests in the choice, often so hard in Germany, between the interests of the community in general and those of the party. No German Minister need give up this cheerful optimism, no matter how sceptically he may regard the parties in the ordinary course of politics. Firm belief in the ultimate victory of the national idea is the first condition of a really national policy. Day and night every German politician should remember the glorious words which Schleiermacher uttered in the dark year of 1807: "Germany is still there, and her invisible strength is unimpaired." This belief we Germans must not forgo in the hurly-burly of our party squabbles, which still makes the display of spontaneous national feeling seem transitory, like a rare hour of rest.

A review of the fate of the German Armament Bills affords at the same time a picture of the changes in the parties with regard to the national idea. The Conservatives have a right to the reputation of never having refused to serve their country, and the National Liberals, too, have never endangered the fate of an Armament Bill. In this respect the old parties of the Cartel hold the foremost place, and it was a loss, not only to them but to the Empire, when the elections of 1890 destroyed their majority and at the same time all prospect of their recovering this majority. Prince Bismarck had bequeathed an Army Bill to the new Reichstag of 1890; this Bill was introduced in a form of much less scope than that of the original draft, as conceived by the old Imperial Chancellor. Count Caprivi asked for 18,000 men and 70 batteries. In spite of the fact that the venerable Moltke spoke in favour of the Bill, its fate was doubtful for a long time. Eugen Richter refused it in the name of the whole Ultra-Liberal party. With the help of the Centre the Bill was passed by the Cartel parties, but the Centre only gave its consent on condition that subsequently a Bill for two-year military service should be introduced.

The great Army Bill of 1893 became a necessity so soon owing to the fact that the demands made by the preceding Bill had been insufficient for requirements; this showed how uncertain the foothold of the national majority of the middle-class parties was. The Centre vented on the Army Bill its resentment for the disappointment of its hopes with regard to educational policy in Prussia. Although its demand for two-year military service was included in the new Bill, the party could not make up its mind to vote for it. Among the Ultra-Liberals the national idea at that time was trying to find expression. But only six Ultra-Liberal deputies at last consented to vote for the Bill. In 1893, sixteen years before its realisation, there rose for a moment the hope of co-operation between the Conservatives and Liberals, including the Ultra-Liberals. The time, however, was not yet ripe. The rejection of the Bill by the Centre, Ultra-Liberals and Social Democrats was followed by the dissolution of the Reichstag. In the elections the Ultra-Liberals in favour of the Army separated from the party of progress; but the elections did not result in a national majority without the Centre. The Social Democrats increased the number of their seats. The bulk of the Ultra-Liberals remained in opposition. The majority—201 against 185—was only obtained by means of the Polish party, which had increased from sixteen to nineteen. The national idea had gained ground among the Ultra-Liberals, but had not won the victory, and had been unable to get ahead of the party interests of the Centre.

Six years later the Government had to put up with

very considerable reductions in its Bills, and nevertheless only succeeded in passing the new Army Bill
with the help of the Centre after a violent struggle
against the opposition of the Ultra-Liberals and Social Democrats. There was no question of ready or
enthusiastic acceptance, and a conflict in home politics
seemed very imminent. I found the majority which
had passed the Tariff Bill ready to accept the Army
increase of 10,000 men in the spring of 1905, but the
Ultra-Liberals still held off. The case was much the
same with the Navy Bills. Hot fights were the rule,
and consent was usually the result of long discussions
and explanations between the Government and the
parties. In the year 1897 not even two cruisers were
granted, and yet in the following year it was possible
to get a majority in the same Reichstag for the first
great Navy Bill.

In the interval, comprehensive and enlightening
work had been done. The Emperor William II. had
advocated the national cause with all his heart and
soul. Learned men like Adolph Wagner, Schmoller,
Sering, Lamprecht, Erich Marks and many others
made successful propaganda for the fleet at that time
and in subsequent years, especially among the educated classes. The Bill of 1898 was passed by a ma-

jority of 212 against 139 votes.   Twenty members of
the Centre, all the Ultra-Liberals and, of course, the
Social Democrats voted against it.   The important
Navy Bill of 1900 again found the Ultra-Liberals
solidly on the side of the Opposition.   The Centre
this time voted as one man for the Bill after the number of cruisers demanded had been reduced from
sixty-four to fifty-one.   In the year 1906 these additional ships, which had been refused before, were
granted by the majority which passed the Tariff Bill.
In the same way the increase in the dimensions of the
battleships, necessitated by the example of England,
was granted.

In the end we certainly succeeded in obtaining majorities of the middle classes for all these Armament
Bills.   But their acceptance was nearly always the
result of difficult negotiations, and often of inconven-
ient compromises.   We were very far from being
able to count on sure and substantial national majorities for our legitimate and reasonable Armament
Bills.   More than once the decision hung in the balance.   And had it not been, as was the case in the
Army Bill of 1893, for the unexpected assistance of
the Poles, success and failure would each time have
been dependent on the presence or absence of the

good will of the Centre. This was bound to give that party not only a very strong sense of power, but a great deal of actual power. The expression, "the all-powerful Centre," so often heard before 1907, was fully justified. In point of fact, a party, on whose good will the Empire was dependent in all questions of national existence, was virtually in possession of political leadership, at least in those matters which, in accordance with the Constitution, are open to the influence of parties and the representatives of the people. And when the Colonial debates of the winter of 1906 showed that it was by no means safe to count on the Centre in all national questions, it became clear that some solution yet remained to be found for the problem of how to safeguard these questions in the party warfare. The change of front of the party of progress, and the victory at the poll of the new majority of the Block, put an end to this rule of the Centre which we have just described. The Centre learnt that the fate of national questions no longer depended on it alone, and it learnt further that the negative attitude might well prove fatal to its powerful position in Parliament. Even though the Block could only be kept together for a few years, yet the possibility remains that it might be formed again

if the Centre should fail to come up to the mark in a
national question, or should, by siding with the Social
Democrats, defeat a Bill for the furtherance of national aims.   The Centre will not be so ready, as it
often was in past years, to allow its attitude with regard to national questions to be influenced by ill-feeling occasioned by matters of home politics.   The
Ultra-Liberals proved, in the spring of 1912 and in
the summer of 1913, that they consider the change of
front carried out in 1906 a permanent one.

That there has been such a development of the national idea, and that such a change has come over
the attitude of the parties towards Imperial questions
of protection and armament, must fill every patriot
with joy and confidence.   Fifty years ago, King William found himself alone with his Ministry and a
small Conservative minority, in the struggle to re-
organise the Prussian Army.   After the founding of
the Empire, Bismarck had to fight obdurately with
the parties for every Army requisition, however small.
The year 1893 witnessed once more a bitter struggle
in home politics for an Army Bill.   In October, 1899,
the Emperor William II. lamented that, "in spite of
urgent requests and warnings" during the first eight
years of his reign, the increase in the Navy had been

steadily refused. When at last the idea of a navy had taken root in the minds of the people, even then the individual Navy Bills were only passed after hard fights in Parliament.

The Armament Bills of 1912 were passed by the whole of the German middle-class parties in the Reichstag. The Army Bill of the year 1913 met with such a willing reception from all parties as had never before been accorded to any requisition for armaments on land or at sea. For the Army Bill itself no serious exposition was really required. If the parties fought over the question of expense, it was for reasons due to the general situation in party politics, and considerations of very serious questions of finance. Not one of the middle-class parties, from the extreme Right to the Ultra-Liberals, even thought of making their consent to the Armament Bill dependent on the difficulties and differences of opinion in the question of meeting expenses. The national idea has taken firm root among all the middle-class parties. As far as man can tell, every necessary and justifiable Army and Navy Bill will always be able to count on a safe parliamentary majority. The period of the Block played a very essential part in the attainment of this success.

ELECTORAL CAMPAIGN AGAINST THE SOCIAL DEMOCRATS.

If the strengthening of the national front rank may be regarded as a permanent result of the parliamentary struggles of the winter of 1906 and of the combination of 1906–1909, then the great electoral victory over the Social Democrats, won in the year 1907, has unfortunately not borne such lasting fruit as it could and should have done.   In spite of this the result of those elections was of very great importance. The fact that the Social Democratic constituencies were reduced from eighty-one and could be reduced to forty-three, has a significance which is not confined to the individual electoral campaign.   The talk about a chance victory is either due to the untruthfulness of party politicians or to regrettable thoughtlessness. Such chance occurrences have no more existence in politics than in life.   In politics, too, every important effect has a corresponding cause.   Such a well organised party as that of the Social Democrats does not lose forty-four constituencies, nor is the number of its seats reduced by thirty-six, without sufficient cause.   Against their forty-four losses in 1907 there were only eight gains.   This success could not be attributed to the national watchword alone. The General Election after the dissolution in 1893 took place under the auspices of a similar watchword, and it resulted in a considerable increase of votes for the extreme Left, and, what is of more practical importance in the course of legislative work, a considerable increase of seats. The cause of the loss of Social Democratic seats in 1907 is to be found in the preliminary work done before that date in Parliament and the Press, by speeches and explanations; in the fact that the right moment was seized to dissolve the Reichstag; in the correct treatment and estimate of imponderables; and in the direction of the electoral campaign.

It is a mistake to under-estimate the value of an electoral triumph over the Social Democrats, because the loss of seats is not accompanied by a corresponding loss of votes. Of course, it would be better not only to gain ground in the Reichstag against the Social Democrats, but also to win over to the national camp a part of their adherents and followers. But this twofold success is difficult to achieve in the meantime, and would only be possible under political circumstances which have not hitherto arisen. Since the year 1884, the number of votes recorded in favour of the Social Democrats has steadily increased. In round numbers the votes recorded are:

1884	550,000
1887	763,000
1890	1,427,000
1893	1,787,000
1898	2,107,000
1903	3,011,000
1907	3,539,000
1912	4,250,000

These figures are doubly instructive. They show the dangerous increase in the number of the supporters of the Social Democrats, and the waning disinclination of the middle-classes to afford them direct support at the elections. But the figures also demonstrate that it is possible to weaken the party of the Social Democrats in the Reichstag in spite of the power of their propaganda. This is clearly shown by the number of the seats they have obtained since 1884:

1884	24
1887	11
1890	35
1893	44
1898	56
1903	81
1907	43
1912	110

These two tables show that a decrease in the votes for the Social Democrats has hitherto not been attainable, but that under suitable guidance it is possible to reduce the number of their seats in the Reichstag. Sound practical policy attends to the achievement of such good as is possible, if for the time being better things are unattainable.

The rise in the number of votes for the Social Democrats is a very serious matter. But as the voting papers have no other immediate object than to gain seats, as the total mass of the supporters and followers of the Social Democrats, huge as it is, can only influence the course of practical legislation if the strength of the Social Democrats in the Reichstag is proportionately increased, the first duty of the Government is to neutralise the effect which the heavy Social Democrat poll has upon the election result. If such a success under the guidance of the Government is secured, not once but repeatedly, then it cannot fail, in the long run, to react on the canvassing and agitation of the Social Democrats. For what is true for all human activity is particularly true in the sphere of politics; nothing has a more paralysing effect than the knowledge that continuous and strenuous effort remains permanently unsuccessful. The prestige of

the Social Democrats is founded largely on a belief
in the irresistible growth of their power. From this
point of view also, the result of the elections of 1907
teaches us a lesson of great and lasting value.

The fact that the Conservatives and Liberals were
on the same side in the principal ballots and the second ballots in 1907, resulted in a very considerable
reduction in Social Democratic seats in spite of the
increase in the Social Democratic vote.

In this respect the Block elections were even more
successful than the Cartel elections in 1887. The
Cartel reduced the Social Democratic seats from
twenty-four to eleven, while the number of Social
Democratic votes increased by nearly a third. At
the Block elections the number of Social Democratic
seats fell from eighty-one to forty-three, while the
votes increased by about a sixth. At the same time,
in the one case the Cartel, and in the other the Block,
obtained a majority in the Reichstag. The loss of
the Social Democrats was the gain of the Conservatives and Liberals. The cause of this is that in
nearly all the constituencies which can be successfully
contested in opposition to the Social Democrats, Liberalism and Conservatism are so strongly represented that their united strength can beat the Social

Democrats, but the latter win the day if Conservatives and Liberals split votes. The point, of course, is to arrange and direct the electoral campaign in such a way that the Conservatives and Liberals can unite. Of the sixty-nine constituencies which the Social Democrats gained in the January elections of 1912, no fewer than sixty-six had returned Conservatives or Liberals in 1907; twenty-nine had fallen to the share of the Conservatives and their neighbours, and thirty-seven to the Liberal parties. The elections of 1907 inflicted the severest loss that the Social Democrats had experienced since the founding of the Reichstag; the elections of 1912 brought them the greatest gain. The parties of the Right fell from the hundred and thirteen seats that they had won in 1907 to sixty-nine in 1912. That is the smallest number of members of the Right since the year 1874. The number of Liberals in the Reichstag after the elections of 1912 was lower than ever before. At the elections of 1907, for the first time, Conservatives and Liberals of all shades of opinion were united for one cause. The elections of 1912 saw a close coalition of all the parties of the Left. In 1907 the Right emerged from the elections as the strongest group, numbering a hundred and thirteen members as against a hundred and six Liberals, a hundred and five representatives of the Centre, and forty-three Socialists. In the year 1912 the Social Democrats were the strongest party in the Reichstag, with a hundred and ten members, while there were ninety representatives of the Centre, eighty-five Liberals, and sixty-nine Conservatives of all shades of opinion.

The comparison between 1907 and 1912 tempts one to ask where the blame lies. I will leave this question unanswered. But the comparison teaches an interesting lesson. It shows that Conservatism cannot find in the assistance of the Centre compensation for the loss occasioned by being completely out of touch with the Left. It shows that the Social Democrats have least chance at elections if the Liberals have been successfully separated from them, and that they achieve their greatest successes when middle-class Liberalism assists them, either voluntarily or because it is driven to do so.

MEANS OF COMBATING THE SOCIAL DEMOCRATS WITH-
OUT RESORTING TO FORCE.

From first to last during my term of office I recognised that the Social Democratic movement constituted a great and serious danger. It is the duty of every German Ministry to combat this movement until it is defeated or materially changed. There can be no doubt as to the task itself, but there may be hesitation as to the choice of means.

Since the law against the Socialists lapsed, suppression by force is no longer feasible. The last time proceedings of this kind were possible was when Prince Bismarck, a man who had won such unparalleled successes, a man of such immense reputation, was at the head of the Government. He could have undertaken and carried out extraordinary measures in home politics, as he was able to do in foreign politics, thanks to his international reputation. Under the political rule of Bismarck much was possible and feasible that must nowadays silently be set down as impracticable. He was a political premise in himself. It is foolish to desire means and enterprises for which this premise is wanting. We must often pursue other courses, and summon up strength and will to reach our goal by their means, without having Bismarck to lead us. This applies also to the fight against the Social Democrats.

Of course every disturbance of public order must be suppressed energetically. That is the first duty of every Government in every civilised State, be it Republican or Monarchical, whether the Government be guided by Conservative, Liberal or Democratic opinions. The resolute way in which in France Ministers belonging to the Radical party with praiseworthy energy suppressed attempts to disturb public order, may well serve as a model for every Minister in other countries. Ill-advised consideration in this respect is a lack of consideration for the great majority of the nation, that has a right to expect to work under the protection of an orderly state of affairs. In accordance with this view, Goethe, who was not so indifferent to political matters as is often supposed, characterised the maintenance of public order as the first duty of every Government. In sympathy with this idea, Schopenhauer, who most certainly was an independent thinker, bequeathed all his fortune to a fund started in Berlin, "for the support of Prussian soldiers disabled in maintaining and restoring public order in Germany during the revolts and disturbances of the years 1848 and 1849." But it is one thing for the Government to proceed by force against disturbances of the peace, and quite another, in order to prevent possible civil disturbances, for it to interfere with the peaceful development of a Radical movement among the people. In the latter case, by employing force, it runs the risk of rousing active resentment which might possibly never have broken out otherwise. Every blow provokes a return blow of corresponding strength. A strong, well-organised political movement in the nation, based on wide and reliable sympathies, will gain in striking power the moment it sees that it is exposed to the danger of being suppressed by force. The recruiting power of a cause is greatly increased if it has the luck, thanks to excess of zeal on the part of its opponents, to be able to point to martyrs to the cause. With regard to this, we need only call to memory the notorious persecutions of demagogues during the second, third and fourth decades of the nineteenth century. By outlawing a number of more or less harmless advocates of democracy the Government gave the democratic movement of those times claims on many classes of the people, which they would certainly not have won over by the power of their ideas alone. The result was the outbreak of 1848.

Of course, it is not possible to say how things would work out in detail nowadays if the Government were to resort to force. The whole situation is very different from that during the first third of the nineteenth century. On the one hand, the modern Social Democratic movement is less good-na-

tured and less idealistic than the middle-class democratic movement before the March Revolution; it
lacks the warm-hearted patriotism of the old German
Democrats; but its economic socialistic aims give it
far more trenchancy and force. On the other hand,
when Prussia was despotically ruled, there was a lack
of the safety valves of parliamentary life, of the
freedom of the Press, and of the right to form Associations and hold meetings—safety valves which are
useful and have become indispensable. Exceptional
laws against the Social Democrats would choke these
outlets. They would force the Social Democratic
movement to transform itself from a strong party
movement into a powerful secret society. Like a
permanent conspiracy, with all the venom, the bit-
terness and the fanaticism, which have hitherto characterised every movement that has been branded by
the Government as unlawful, the party would only
become welded together more firmly; but, as far as
the Government and the people are concerned, the
open enemy whose methods can be controlled would
become a secret foe, whose courses it would not always be possible to trace.

If the Government decides to use forcible means,
it deprives itself of all possibility of perhaps effecting

more by peaceful methods.   Force can only be used
as the very last resource.   It only comes into question when all peaceful methods obviously have failed.
So far this is not the case.   If once the Government
embarks on a course of violence there can be no turn-
ing back, for that would mean a confession of defeat.   If the means which law and justice place at
our disposal fail, the last resource still remains.   No
good general calls up his reserves at the beginning of
an engagement, he keeps them back so that if the
battle takes a critical turn he may not be defence-
less.   These excellent military tactics are of equal
value in political struggles.   Those are the best political successes that are won with least sacrifice.   In
case of need the strongest measures are the best.
But they should not be used without urgent necessity,
and, above all, without the certainty that they will be
successful.   Bismarck could break all rules, and could
expect success from an extreme and bold action.   We
cannot do so to-day, and are obliged to depend on un-
tiring and steady endeavour.   Of course it is within
the province of such endeavour fearlessly to apply
the laws which serve to maintain order, safety and
liberty, and if they should prove insufficient in individual points, to supplement them.

Forcible proceedings against the Social Democrats would immediately come into question if they were provoked by any violent outburst of the Social Democratic movement. That, however, is hardly to be expected and is improbable, if the Goverment attacks the problem of dealing with the Social Democrats skilfully and performs its task energetically. There are politicians who think it would be no misfortune if a violent outburst took place, because then there would be a possibility of cutting the Gordian knot of the Socialist question with the sword and thus attaining a final solution.

If the Social Democrats should be stupid and criminal enough to resort to open rebellion, then, of course, all considerations and all doubts would have to be discarded, in the face of the necessity of defending the foundations of our State and our civilisation. But to desire such a development of affairs is shortsighted. I once expressed in the Reichstag what consideration a policy deserves that wishes for a violent outburst in the country, or even goes the length of provoking it in the hope of arriving at better conditions by suppressing it forcibly. In France forty years ago it was called *"politique de la mer Rouge."* The Red Sea was to be crossed in order to reach the

Promised Land. Only, unfortunately, there is great danger of drowning in the Red Sea and never reaching the Promised Land. A large proportion of the French Monarchists acted in pursuance of this recipe, when the preliminary signs of the great Revolution increased in number. Instead of coming to an agreement with the moderate men, they persecuted them with bitter animosity, and preferred to favour the extremists indirectly, in the hope thereby of bringing about the deluge, after which they would be in clover. The deluge came, but they were not in clover. The attempt to set a thief to catch a thief has rarely succeeded in politics.

Germany is not the country for a *coup d'état*. No people in the world has such a strong sense of law as the Germans. Nowhere does the infringement of a law, whether of common law or of public equity, produce such passionate resentment as in Germany, nor is there any nation which finds it so hard to forget such a breach as we do. The objection of most German parties to exceptional laws and exceptional expedients is also due to their innate dislike of breaking the law. The French are less sensitive on this point. The supporters of the Great Revolution still glory in its terrorism. Thiers, in the seventh volume of his "History of the French Revolution," in considering the Reign of Terror of the National Convention, concludes with the words: "Le souvenir de la Convention Nationale est demeuré terrible; mais pour elle il n'y a qu'un fait à alléguer, un seul, et tous les reproches tombent devant ce fait immense: elle nous a sauvés de l'invasion étrangère." * M. Clémenceau was of opinion that the Revolution, with all its excesses and infringement of the law, must be taken *en bloc* and be considered as a whole. The *coup d'état* of Napoleon I. was forgotten when the sun of Austerlitz rose over the Empire. Napoleon III., too, was only reminded again of December 2 when he made great blunders in foreign policy, and only after Sedan "Rue du 2 Décembre" was changed to "Rue du 4 Septembre."

NO POLICY OF CONCILIATION.

Every page of German history, on the contrary, tells how stubbornly the German defends his good old law, how irreconcilable he is, when old law is discarded to make way for sound and necessary progress. Law must certainly not be considered superior to the

* "The memory of the National Convention remains a terrible one, but there is only one fact to urge in its favour, and all reproaches fall to the ground before this immense fact: it saved us from foreign invasion."

needs of the State. *Fiat jus et pereat mundus* does not apply to politics. But so long as the needs of the State can be satisfied on the basis of the law this must be done. Also in the fight against the Social Democrats. If they openly break the law they must be paid back in their own coin. Such a turn of affairs must be reckoned with, but it must not be desired or forced. Forcible remedies without healing powers have never yet produced permanent results. On the other hand, in view of German conditions, and especially those in Prussia, the Social Democratic party, with its present programme and aims, cannot be placed on the same level as those parties which take their stand on the existing political system. A comparison with other countries which have succeeded, or seem gradually to be succeeding, in making the Socialist party participate in the Government of the country does not hold good in view of German conditions. We have a different political system, and, above all, different Social Democrats. Here again the warning of Bismarck applies, that we must not seek our models abroad, if we lack the conditions and qualities necessary for the imitation of foreign institutions.

In France the Socialists have become Ministers,

and good Ministers too, and have shown how right is the French proverb which says, "qu'un Jacobin ministre n'est pas toujours un ministre jacobin." Aristide Briand, once a Radical Socialist, proved himself a determined guardian of public order; the Social Democrat, Millerand, was an excellent Minister of War.

In Italy, too, the attempt to make the Socialists share in the Government has succeeded. In Holland and Denmark similar attempts have probably been only temporarily abandoned. In a large number of other counties it will probably not be long before the French and Italian examples of a gradual reconciliation with the Socialist element will be imitated.

We must not be deceived by the apparently favourable results of such experiments. Just as our past, our political development and our peculiarities differ from those of other countries, so does our Social Democratic problem. We must study our own conditions, the peculiarities of the German Social Democrats, who attack the foundations of our State, and the peculiarities of our State, which we must defend against the Social Democrats.

The strong points of our national character, as well

as its weak ones, come to light in the Social Democratic movement. The movement, as it stands at
present, would be an impossibility in any country of
the world except Germany. It is so dangerous to
us because it is so typically German. No other nation has such a gift for organisation, no nation sub-
mits so willingly to discipline, or has the power to
subordinate itself to such an extent to strict discipline.
We owe our best successes to this gift, our most useful
public institutions. The Prussian State was created
by discipline, as were our Army and our Public Services. That which other nations did in the heat of
enthusiasm we often achieved by the power of discipline. The war of 1866 was not popular; the troops
were not urged on by patriotic enthusiasm, as was the
case half a century earlier, but started on their march
to Bohemia in silent submission to the orders of the
commanding officers, and under the rule of discipline
achieved victories as glorious as were those of their
fathers under the inspiration of enthusiasm. After
the war, a Frenchman wrote in admiration: "That
the war in Bohemia had shown what could be achieved
by strength of discipline alone." It is one of the German's greatest political virtues that discipline is bred
in his bone. But the Social Democrats make use of

this virtue.   Only in a State where the people are used to discipline, where they have learnt to obey unquestioningly in the Army, and where they feel the rigid regulations of the administrative machinery daily and hourly, could a party organisation of such size and solidarity as that of the Social Democrats come into being.   The way the 4,216 local Societies submit to the forty-eight country and district Associations, and these again to the Central Association; the way enormous subscriptions are paid as if they were lawful taxes; the way the huge demonstrations are arranged, as if they were military operations; all this is not the result only of enthusiasm for a political party, it is also due to the sense of discipline which the German has in his blood.   No nation in the world possesses or has ever possessed a like or even a similar party organisation.   The clubs of the Jacobins, which were spread like a network over France, were only a pale prototype of our Social Democratic organisation.   The provincial Clubs obeyed the Paris Central Association only so long as this was a power in the State, and were closed later on, without difficulty, at a hint from the Directoire Government.   The strong web of the German Social Democratic party would not be so easy to tear.

The late ambassador in St. Petersburg, General von Schweinitz, once said to me: "There are only two absolutely perfect organisations in the world: the Prussian Army and the Catholic Church." As far as organisation alone is concerned, one might be tempted to bestow similar praise on the German Social Democratic party. In one of my Reichstag speeches—it was in December, 1903—I said, in this connection: "If I had to make out a report for the Social Democratic movement, I should say: Criticism, agitation, discipline and self-sacrifice, Ia; positive achievements, lucidity of programme, Vb." * This organisation of the Social Democrats is definitely hostile to our political system, and looks on this hostility as its bond of union. There is no possibility of reconciling them to the State and of dissolving them in so doing, by tying them for a time to the Government cart, or allowing this member or the other to take part in the direction of affairs. The movement is far too strong to allow itself, so to speak, to be coupled like a truck to the Government locomotive, and to let itself be pulled along a definite track; it would want to be a locomotive itself, and would try to pull in the opposite direction. The Social Democrats would not obey a man

* Ia, the best, and Vb, the worst marks in a school report.

from their midst who, in existing circumstances, should take service as a Minister any more than any other German party has ever done.

To this must be added that the dogmatic trait, so characteristic of the German people, is also strongly expressed in our Social Democratic party. The German Social Democrat clings tenaciously to the tenets of his party, tenaciously and uncritically, and caring nothing for the inner contradictions of the Social Democratic programme. And as this programme is incompatible with the existing State, the German Social Democrats are irreconcilable. The German working men, more than the same class in any other country, are inclined to believe implicitly in the Socialistic principles and the brilliant sophisms of Lassalle, and in the system of Marx, the construction of which affords proof of tremendous mental power and rare perspicacity, of extraordinary knowledge and still more extraordinary dialectics, but which, in the course of historical development, has been refuted and shaken to its foundations. When Giolitti reproached the Italian Socialists with having discarded the tenets of Marx, he only evoked intelligent amusement. An apostrophe of that kind in our country would have been met with indignant protests. Our Social Demo-

cratic party is of the school of Eisenach; not Lassalle
and Rodbertus, but Marx and Engels, Bebel and
Liebknecht have been its guides, and its attitude towards the State is incomparably more hostile than
that of the Socialist parties in France and Italy, which
attribute a more or less academic value to Socialistic
theories, and which are founded, not only on the Socialistic idea, but also on national memories. French
Socialism really springs from the Great Revolution,
and the Revolution, like the Risorgimento, was inspired by a passionately patriotic spirit.

Our Social Democratic party lacks this national
basis. It will have nothing to do with German patriotic memories which bear a monarchical and military character. It is not, like the French and Italian
parties, a precipitate of the process of national historical development, but since its existence it has been
in determined opposition to our past history as a nation. It has placed itself outside our national life.
Whatever is achieved and accomplished in the State
is of no interest to it, except in so far as it can serve
to crush existing conditions, and in that manner clear
the way for the realisation of purely Socialistic ideas.
In the calendar that the *Vorwärts* publishes every
year, Bismarck and Moltke, Blücher and Scharnhorst,

Ziethen and Seidlitz are not mentioned, nor are Leipzig and Waterloo, Königgrätz and Sedan, but a series
of Russian Nihilists and Italian Anarchists and their
murderous enterprises are named.

Just as one of the greatest German virtues, the
sense of discipline, finds special and disquieting expression in the Social Democratic movement, so does
our old vice, envy. *Propter invidiam,* said Tacitus
about our ancestors; the Germans destroyed their lib-
erators, the Cherusci. Envy is one of the main-
springs of our Social Democratic movement. Economic contrasts have been intensified just as much in
other countries as with us. The violent exasperation
roused thereby in Germany is found nowhere else,
in spite of the fact that so much has been accomplished in social reform, and although Germany led
the way in making provision for the poor, and is still
in advance of all other countries in this respect. The
struggle of the labouring classes for better conditions
of life, which originated at the time of the inception
of the Social Democratic movement, has grown at
times in Germany to a fanatical hatred of property
and culture, birth and position. The excellent arrangements to raise the status of the workmen have
not had much effect on this envy. Daily fanned into

fresh flame by the sight of the contrast between rich and poor, this envy would not vanish if some leader or other took his seat on the Ministerial Bench. The Social Democratic movement has become a reservoir for this envy.

The German Social Democrats cling most lovingly, and with tenacious obstinacy, to the ultimate goal of Socialism, the destruction of differences in wealth by the suppression of private property and the national-isation of the means of production. The Social Dem-ocrats, too, will not be won over by a policy of recon-ciliation, *propter invidiam*. And finally, the objec-tionable German caste-feeling which stands in the way of natural social intercourse, and which has an adverse influence on our whole political life, finds its ultimate and bitterest expression in Social Demo-cratic class-hatred. The old classes, historic in origin, had been delimited by public and legal circumstances. The Social Democratic proletariat, with its class-hatred, created itself, and has thrown up a dividing wall between itself and the rest of its fellow country-men. It will have nothing in common with the other classes of society. And, as with every caste, the So-cial Democratic proletariat not only considers itself better, more useful and more competent than other classes of the nation, but it also aims at dominating all the other classes. If the attempt were made amongst us to bring the Social Democratic party into line with the middle-class parties, it is very questionable whether the Social Democrats would consent. They feel they have a vocation for autocratic rule, and will hardly content themselves with a proportionate share in the Government.

THE PRUSSIAN STATE AND THE SOCIAL DEMOCRATS.

In the German Empire, Prussia is the leading State. The Social Democratic movement is the antithesis of the Prussian State. A well-known proposition of Hegel's maintains that every idea includes its reverse counter idea. It is most significant that the philosopher who called the State the present deity, whose legal philosophy was a glorification of the Prussian State, who rejoiced in the special protection of the highest Prussian State authorities, should have created the logical premises for the conclusions of Marx.

The peculiarity of the Prussian State, which is the backbone of our political life, makes a solution of the Social Democratic problem particularly difficult for us. The practical *modus vivendi* with the Social

Democrats, that has been attempted here and there in Southern Germany, does not seem possible in Prussia. Prussia attained her greatness as a country of soldiers and officials, and as such she was able to accomplish the work of German union; to this day she is still in all essentials a State of soldiers and officials. The strong control exercised by the authorities in Prussia has always evoked a particularly vigorous counter movement. The Berlin mania for grumbling and criticism was well known throughout Germany in the times of the absolute monarchy, when Frederick the Great had the pamphlets hung lower. Only civil authorities, who were as greatly used to guidance as the Prussians were, could lose their heads so completely as they did in the disastrous year of 1806, when control slipped out of the hands of the Government. Even after the transition to constitutional forms of Government the Democracy in Prussia remained far more hostile than in the South, and went further in its demands. In consequence, the reaction in Prussia in the 'fifties was particularly severe. The Social Democrats, who in South Germany often adopt a conciliatory attitude and are ready to forgo some of the demands of the Socialistic programme for the sake of the practical politics of the day, are in Prussia as extreme in their attitude as in their demands. As a natural contrast to this, Prussia has a far stronger Conservative element than any other German State possesses or needs. The Prussian State may be compared to a man, and, like any man worth his salt, is full of violent contrasts and only capable of great achievements when animated by a strong purpose. At home and abroad this State has mostly been very strong or very weak. Deeds of great strength and deeds of great weakness are found here in close proximity. Jena and Leipzig are only seven years apart. The sad retreat of the troops from Berlin on March 19, 1848, and the weak-kneed policy which led back by way of Bronzell and Olmütz to the old Federal Diet, were followed twenty years later by Sadowa and Sedan. Under powerful authority, Prussia was stronger in herself and had a more devoted and better disciplined population than any other State. But when the authorities became weak and disheartened, timid and neutral in the expression of their will, Prussia experienced a more complete breakdown of her State machinery than any other country. The authorities were hopelessly incompetent, when in 1806 the Minister for Home Affairs declared peacefulness to be the first duty of the people, though the country lay at the mercy of the enemy, and the officials of Berlin humbly welcomed the conqueror at the Brandenburg Gate; so were they, too, in the year of revolution, 1848, when the Lord Lieutenant of the Province of Saxony declared proudly that he took up his stand above all parties, while a mighty party movement was shaking the foundations of the monarchy. If the Prussian Government wanted to come to terms with the Social Democrats, and was willing to recognise as legitimate the demands of a party which for decades has been combating the monarchical and military foundations of the Prussian State, the Prussian civil servants, the middle-classes, the country population East of the Elbe, and possibly the army itself, would be at a loss what to make of the State and the authorities. If the Government renounced the fight against the Social Democrats, Prussia would take it to mean that they had yielded to the forces of revolution. And they would be right, if, after half a century of fighting, the Government could find no other solution than a shameful peace with the enemy. The results of a weak attitude towards the Social Democrats to-day would be more fatal in Prussia than weakness towards the March Revolution was. And it is very questionable whether another Bismarck could be found to restore the authority of the Crown which had been weakened, not by defeats, but first by irresolution and indulgent forbearance, and then by stupid and foolish retrograde action.

For the Prussian official, the Prussian soldier and the Prussian civilian, whose views are rooted in Prussian traditions, confidence in the strength of the Government is a necessary condition of devoted loyalty. An agreement with the Social Democrats, which might be interpreted as an act of political wisdom in South Germany, would in Prussia be synonymous with a triumph of the Social Democrats over the Government and over the Crown.

The immediate consequence would be an enormous increase in the membership of the Social Democratic party. In Prussia loyalty to the King, which is bred in the bone of the Prussian and bequeathed to him by remote ancestors, keeps many back from joining the Social Democrats. But hundreds of thousands would follow without scruple a Social Democratic party which had acquired almost royal privileges. Instead of winning over the party to the interests of the State, in Prussia thousands of good subjects, in a state of bewilderment as regards their political ideas, would be driven to the side of the Social Democrats.

The party would emerge from such an agreement, not weakened but strengthened, and it would not dream of approaching the State in earnest, or of changing for the sake of the State, since the latter was ready to meet it half way in any case. In Prussia the experiment of coming to terms could only be possible if the Social Democratic party had first publicly, and in full form, made its peace with the monarchy. Until that has come to pass the Prussian Government cannot attempt a policy of conciliation as regards the Social Democratic party without fear of destroying the State. The Social Democrats hate the Kingdom of the Eagle, "which dips one wing in the Niemen and the other in the Rhine." They hate Prussia as being a State of orderly organisation, the heart and core of the German Empire, the State without which the German Empire would not exist, whose kings united Germany, with which the future of the Empire stands or falls.

Bebel's words, that if the Social Democrats had won Prussia they would have won all, are perfectly true. But it is also true that Prussia is difficult, if not impossible, for them to win if they have to fight against a strong Government, but that with the aid of the Government no German State would so easily be conquered by the Social Democrats as Prussia.

The peculiarities of Prussian conditions must, of course, react on the Empire. It is impossible to come to an agreement for any length of time with the Social Democrats on important questions of Imperial legislation, and yet to retain a violent antagonism to the Social Democrats in Prussia. The Reichstag elections cannot be carried on from an absolutely different standpoint from that of the Prussian Diet elections. The Social Democrats will hardly be willing to come to an arrangement in the Empire so long as they are opposed in Prussia. On the other hand, an attempt on the part of the Imperial Government to make an agreement would have the same confusing and disintegrating effect on Prussia as a similar attempt in that State itself. If the Empire is governed without reference to Prussia, ill-will towards the Empire will grow in that country. If Prussia is governed without reference to the Empire, then there is the danger that mistrust and dislike of the leading State will gain ground in non-Prussian Germany. It has always been disastrous for Prussia if necessary reforms, instead of being undertaken in time, were stubbornly refused until at last, by force of circumstances, they had to be granted in an ex-

treme form. The art of governing in our country
will always have to be directed chiefly towards maintaining the harmony between Germany and Prussia
in the spirit as well as in the letter.

The peculiarity of the conditions in our State, as
well as the character of our Social Democratic party,
are both equally opposed to a policy of conciliation.
Forcible suppression of the Social Democratic movement is out of the question. By these two direct
methods no solution of the Social Democratic problem, no exorcism of the danger which threatens us,
is possible. The only hope is to attack the causes
and the forces which inspire the Social Democratic
movement.

ISOLATION OF THE SOCIAL DEMOCRATIC MOVEMENT.

The Social Democratic movement is revolutionary
in character. It is a question whether it will proceed
to revolutionary deeds. Its aims, which involve a
fundamental change of our whole public life, are revolutionary *sans phrase*. Consequently for this movement those experiences are applicable which have been
gathered in every other revolutionary movement. History shows that a radical tendency rarely grows more
moderate without some external cause. New fol-

lowers which a Radical party obtains rarely have a moderating influence for any length of time; rather they tend to enhance the striking power, and are liable to submit with increasing docility to Radical leadership. As in every party, the extreme section of the Social Democratic party has taken command in decisive moments because they seemed to have the clearest perception.

The opinion is often expressed that the Social Democratic party will grow less dangerous and calmer as members of the educated classes join it. Such a belief is contrary to all experience. The educated men in the Social Democratic movement do not form a bridge by which the proletariat may approach the representatives of the existing order, but a bridge by which intellect passes over to the masses. But it is when the educated classes join a revolutionary movement that it becomes a serious danger.

History teaches us that such movements can be victorious when the temper of the intellectuals, of middle-class intelligence, makes them unite with the masses in their desires. Thus it was in the Great Revolution. So long as the superior insight, the strong will of a Mirabeau kept the Liberal bourgeoisie attached to the monarchy and aloof from the

Jacobins, a peaceful transition of France to the forms of a constitutional kingdom lay within the bounds of possibility. When, after his death, the Gironde obtained ascendancy and the bourgeoisie united with the town mobs against the supporters of the old régime and the Constitutional Monarchists, the fate of the Monarchy and of old France was sealed, and sealed for ever. In 1830 the legitimate Monarchy, scarcely fifteen years after it had been restored, succumbed to a like coalition between intellect and brute force. The March Revolution of 1848 was successful because the masses found support and guidance in the educated classes. Wherever the proletariat has fought alone, as in the June battle in Paris and during the Commune, it has always been defeated. An isolated proletariat, however numerous, is always a minority in the nation. Against the four million Social Democratic voters in 1912 may be set the eight million who did not vote for the Social Democrats. If left to its own resources the proletariat cannot attain a numerical majority in the nation. It can only do so if aided by the middle classes. This is what must primarily be prevented. The Social Democratic party can only be isolated if Liberalism is kept away from it and is drawn towards the Government and the Right.   But that cannot be accomplished by unctuous warnings to Liberalism sedulously to avoid its Radical neighbour.   The separation of Liberalism from the Social Democratic movement can only be accomplished in the course of practical politics by a suitable grouping of the parties.   This task of separating the Social Democratic party from the intelligent middle class is one reason why Ministers whose inner convictions are quite, or, at any rate, largely, Conservative must rule in such a way as not to repel Liberalism.

THE SOCIAL DEMOCRATIC MOVEMENT AND THE WORKMEN.

Socialistic dreams are bound to have something very attractive about them for the workman, so often in needy circumstances, and struggling hard for the livelihood of his family and himself.

My predecessor in office, Prince Hohenlohe, used to call Socialism the poor man's dream. The unschooled judgment of a simple man must easily succumb to the seductive sophistry of Socialist teachings. The Social Democrats raise great hopes among, and hold out dazzling promises to, the workmen, and the glamour is so strong that they cling tenaciously to the idea. It is an old truth that men grasp nothing more closely than their hopes, and that if given the choice of great hope or small fulfilment they choose the former.

We must not cease, therefore, to impress upon our countrymen of the working class the truth of the facts that Socialist promises are illusory, and that Socialism will not accomplish the great miracle of doing away with poverty, care and the industrial struggle; that the actual provisions for the poor made by the existing State and existing society are worth more than the promises of the Social Democrats which can never be fulfilled. We must fight steadily for the souls of our workmen, must seek to win back the Social Democratic workman to the State and the monarchy, and to keep the non-Social Democratic workman away from the danger of imbibing such views. A large number of workmen have not yet succumbed to the attractions of the Social Democrats. As opposed to the 2,530,390 working men in the so-called free or Social Democratic Trades Unions, there are 1,314,799 in non-Social Democratic Trades Unions and Associations. These are as follows:

Catholic Working Men's Union	545,574
Evangelical Working Men's Union	180,000
Christian Trades Unions	360,000

State Workmen's and State Employees' Association .. 120,000
Hirsch-Duncker Trades Unions 109,225

To these must be added the Catholic and Evangelical
Journeymen's Unions and Lads' Unions, whose total
membership numbers 468,223, and, above all, the
great number of industrial and agricultural labourers
who are not organised in unions.   Thanks to the work
of the Lads' Brigade, and of the *Jungdeutschland-
bund* (Union of Young Germany), a valuable start
has been made towards safeguarding the young
people from the Social Democrats' attempts at recruiting.   Even though the Social Democratic organisation is very strong, yet already there are organisations in process of formation, or of growing power,
which, with skilful handling, may be used as a basis
for a successful fight against the Social Democrats;
and other organisations can also be formed.   The
monarchy which, as I explained in the Reichstag on
January 20, 1903, at the beginning of last century
made the transition from the old form of government
to the new without any violent upheaval, is still strong
enough and has sufficient insight to mitigate and re-
move, as far as is possible in this imperfect world, those
evils which, together with much good, are due to modern development, evils which are found in all countries,

and which are comprehended in the words, "social problems." We must not waver in this belief in spite of, or rather because of, the strong attraction that the Social Democratic movement has for our German workmen.

Our fight against the Social Democrats is not directed against the workmen; its aim is to rescue them from the snares of the Social Democrats, and to accustom them to the idea of the State. We must not respond to the Social Democratic hatred of the propertied and educated classes, by hatred of the workmen who have succumbed to the wiles of the Social Democratic propaganda. We remember that the workman is our fellow countryman. In him we also honour God's image. And what we do to relieve his distress we do not only for political reasons, but from a sense of duty and in pursuance of God's command. Since the beginning of the new century we have continued and in part completed the magnificent structure of our social legislation, not because we have such a strong Social Democratic party, but in spite of that fact. The clearer our conscience towards the working classes, because with a social policy on such a large scale we have done all that is humanly possible to alleviate their economic conditions, the better is our right to take up the battle necessitated by reasons of State against the Social Democrats and their political aims.

Catholics have merited much praise for having, to a very large extent, restrained Catholic workmen from joining the Social Democratic movement. But that the Church possesses no secret cure for revolutionary movements is proved by the history of France and Italy, and of Spain and Portugal. In our country the Conservative elements cannot rely on the Church party alone for support, if only for the reason that here, where Protestantism predominates, and where education is imbued mainly with the Protestant spirit, a majority consisting of Conservatives and the Centre alone would be a very narrow one, and, moreover, one to which there attaches the danger that it might lead to a coalition of all the elements of the Left. That would only bring about what must be prevented, namely, that middle-class intellectuals would be brought more and more into touch with the Social Democratic movement.

A VIGOROUS NATIONAL POLICY THE TRUE REMEDY AGAINST THE SOCIAL DEMOCRATIC MOVEMENT.

The true means of restraining the majority of the nation from pursuing the revolutionary aims of the

Social Democrats and from adopting the seductive belief of the Socialists in an infinitely better future, is to pursue a courageous, wide-minded policy which can maintain the nation's satisfaction in the present conditions of life—a policy which brings the best powers of the nation into play; which supports and strengthens the middle classes, already numerous and ever increasing in number, the vast majority of whom steadily uphold the monarchy and the State; which, without bureaucratic prejudices, opens a State career to men of talent; and which appeals to the better feelings of the nation. The idea of the nation as such must again and again be emphasised by dealing with national problems, so that this idea may continue to move, to unite and to separate the parties.

Nothing has a more discouraging, paralysing and depressing effect on a clever, enterprising and highly developed nation such as the Germans, than a monotonous, dull policy which, for fear of an ensuing fight, avoids rousing passions by strong action. My predecessor in office, Prince Chlodwig Hohenlohe, was for long a very kind chief to me when he was ambassador in Paris, and he often conversed with me even when we were not on duty. Once, when he was praising a certain Bavarian statesman as being particularly capable, diligent and conscientious, I asked him why, as President of the Bavarian Ministry, he had not proposed this man for a Ministerial post. "He was not reckless enough for a Minister," replied the Prince very gravely. When I expressed my surprise that such a thoughtful, calm and exceedingly prudent man as Prince Hohenlohe could say such a thing, the wise and politic Prince answered: "You must not understand my remark as an encouragement to reckless action in life, to which young people incline only too readily. What I said was meant politically. A Minister must have a good amount of resolution and energy in his character. He must sometimes risk a big stake and ride at a high hurdle, otherwise he will never be any good."

Various similar remarks of Prince Bismarck's might be adduced in support of this one of Prince Hohenlohe's. Governments and Ministers must not avoid struggles. A sound nation has even more need of friction between itself and the Government than of friction between the parties. This friction produces the vivifying warmth, without which the political life of a people ultimately grows dull. It is a curious fact that the German has always felt the need of occasionally knocking up against the authorities. Nothing annoys him more than if the authorities get out of the way. And it will always be found that party antagonism is most intensified when the Government is disinclined to do battle now and again. The old German delight in fighting, of which we hear in history and legend, still lives on in our political life. A German considers that policy the best which does not leave him in peace, but which keeps him busy fighting and allows him occasionally to display his prowess; in a word, a policy which by its own vigour invigorates him.

True, there is a difference between a political fight and political vexation. The former is vivifying, the latter venomous. The people are well able to perceive whether the Government proves its power in great matters, or abuses it in small ones. It is the same with the master of the State as with the master of the home. A home tyrant is mostly a weakling; strong-willed men are usually broad-minded and indulgent in little things at home, because they use their strength for great things. By a policy of pin-pricks a Government only makes itself unpopular without earning respect. Nothing more easily produces discontent with existing conditions, nothing tends more to foster Radicalism among the people than narrow-minded bureaucracy, clumsiness on the part of the police, and, above all, interference in intellectual matters, in which a civilised nation quite rightly wishes to remain unmolested.

It is not a specifically German quality, but one common to all mankind, that personal experience of injustice, and of vexation at mistakes on the part of the administration, lives more vividly and more permanently in the memory than the most reasonable political conviction.

Their name is legion who, for such reasons, oppose the State and the authorities by means of Social Democratic voting papers. Social Democrats suck the finest honey from the flower of bureaucracy. It is only by living abroad that one can appreciate thoroughly what Germany, and especially Prussia, owes to her civil service, which has been built up by great rulers and excellent Ministers out of the precious material of German loyalty and conscientiousness, love of work and power to work, and has achieved great things in all spheres. If, when a German returns home, the country from the Alps to the Baltic and from the Maas to the Memel lies before him like a well-tended garden, the merit is in no small measure due to the civil service.

The more this service keeps free from our ancestral faults of pedantry and caste-feeling, while preserving its traditional advantages, the wider its outlook; the more humane its attitude in intercourse with all classes of the population; the more enlightened its views, the greater will be its achievements in the future. Indulgence and freedom from prejudice in small things can well be combined with ruthless energy in great ones. Just because our Social Democratic movement is so strong and dangerous, it is necessary that the people should learn to distinguish between the sphere of civil freedom that must be administered with indulgence and the sphere of public State dominion that must be ruled with strength and firmness. However misleading a comparison between German and foreign conditions is in general, here is a field in which England may serve as a model and an example to be imitated. In England every disturbance of public order is ruthlessly suppressed; but chicanery, which interferes with the liberty and comfort of the individual, is avoided with scrupulous care. Ill-grace on the part of the State, so common in Germany, is almost unknown in England. But the Englishman is such a good subject of the State in no small degree because the State gives him such liberty in his private life. The limits of State control, which in our country are still ill-defined, are perfectly definite in England.

No one can believe to-day that the Social Democratic movement will cease to exist within a measurable time, or to be a power and a great danger in our public life. But the fight against it is not hopeless. The Social Democrats are quite vulnerable in their parliamentary position. The elections of 1907 proved how hard they may be hit. The Social Democratic movement can be confined to the proletariat, and, according to all historical experience, robbed of all prospect of ultimate victory, if we can succeed in keeping it out of the middle classes. If the State treats the workman justly and without prejudice; if it makes it easy for him to feel that he enjoys the full rights of a citizen, and does his duty in social matters, then it must and will be possible to solve the labour problem in accordance with the national idea. Through the apparently insignificant but really very efficacious means of skilful and broad-minded government it is possible to stem the stream of Social Democratic recruits. Finally, ruthless energy in suppressing any attempt to disturb public order can make it obvious to the Social Democrats that any schemes of that kind, even on a big scale, are hopeless. So long as the Social Democrats do not fulfil the conditions, which I laid down nearly eleven years ago, as an indispensable preliminary to any adjustment of the differences between them and us; so long as they do not act with sense and in accordance with the laws, do not make their peace with the monarchical form of government, do not cease to wound feelings that are sacred to the great majority of the German nation; so long as they remain as they are now, it will be the duty of the Government to combat them.

The Government must not leave this battle to the parties, it must fight it itself. For the Social Democratic movement does not only threaten the existence of one party or another; it is a danger to the country and the monarchy. This danger must be faced and met with a great and comprehensive national policy, under the strong guidance of clear-sighted and courageous Governments which, whether amicably or by fighting, can make the parties bow to the might of the national idea.

III

ECONOMIC POLICY

Seldom, if ever, has a country experienced such a tremendous economic development in such a short time as the German Empire in the period from the Peace of Frankfurt to the present day. The consolidation of Germany's position as a Great Power of Europe, with the resultant union of the German States and safeguarding of the German frontiers, and the entry into the realm of world-policy accompanied by the construction of a strong fleet: these two significant political events of our modern history most directly benefited the development of our industrial life.

ECONOMIC GROWTH AND DEVELOPMENT OF INDUSTRY.

During more than forty years of peace the German spirit of enterprise awoke for the first time since the end of the Middle Ages, and was able to make use of the rapid spread of means of communication, the achievements of technical science and skill, the great development of the modern circulation of money, to work for the increase of German prosperity. The poor German country has become a rich country. The nation of thinkers, poets and soldiers has become a nation of merchants and shopkeepers of the first rank, and to-day in the world's markets disputes the prize with England, who was already the first commercial nation of the world at a time when the German outlook was still that of peasants and artisans. Where are the times when Schiller saw only two nations struggling for the possession of the world—the Frank, who throws his iron sword into the scale of justice, and the Briton, who sends forth his mercantile fleet like the arms of a polypus—when he transported the German, who had lingered in the realm of dreams while the earth was divided up, together with the poor poet, into the heaven of idealistic simplicity?

To-day German industry has its customers even in the remotest corners of the earth. The German merchant flag is a familiar sight in foreign ports, and knows that it is protected by the German Navy. German capital is employed abroad together with that of the old financial Powers, England and France, and contributes to the consolidation of the industrial ties between us and other nations. The consequences of our national regeneration have hitherto been most apparent in the sphere of the world's industries. In the statistics of international traffic and commerce the rise of the German Empire beside the old Powers is most plastically expressed.

We have reason to be proud of our mighty industrial successes, and the satisfaction of the German patriot is justified, if he points out in what an extraordinarily short space of time we Germans in our economic development have covered the ground which half a century ago separated us from nations that we have now outstripped.

Such success is only possible to the exuberant vitality of a nation thoroughly sound, strong of will and full of ambition. But we must not conceal from ourselves the fact that the almost furious speed of our industrial ascent often hindered calm organic development, and created discords which demanded adjustment. On account of striking successes, due to a special talent, men are prone to neglect the harmonious development of other abilities and powers. At times they may have to pay for such one-sidedness by a painful set-back, if altered circumstances demand other powers and achievements. In Germany the rapid economic development produced a speedy blossoming of industry and commerce under the sun of happy circumstances. The perfected means of communication opened for us in a very different manner from what was possible before, the markets of even the remotest countries. The treasures of our home soil had been left untouched, the incomparable progress in mechanical and electrical engineering placed at our disposal new industrial machinery, and the quick growth of our population provided the masses of workmen for the foundation and expansion of great industrial undertakings. In addition to this, forty years of peace afforded an opportunity for working the world's markets in every direction. The commercial and industrial talent of the German nation, which once before, centuries ago, had made us the first commercial and trading nation of the world, and which, owing to the atrophy of our State and a hard national struggle for existence had been held in abeyance till the last years of the nineteenth century, was extraordinarily favoured by circumstances. When employers and princely merchants like Stumm and Krupp, Ballin and Rathenau, Kirdorf and Borsig, Gwinner and Siemens were found to take advantage of these favourable condi-

tions, the successes of the immediate future were bound
to fall to industry and commerce. The nation turned
more and more towards the new prospects opening
before it. The lower classes deserted the land and
flowed in a stream into industrial undertakings. The
middle and upper classes of the commonalty provided
a large number of capable industrial officials.

The industrialisation which had given signs of
growth in the middle of the nineteenth century, was
accomplished in Germany after the founding of the
Empire, and especially after the end of the 'eighties,
with a vehemence which has only been equalled in
the United States. In the year 1882, agriculture still
employed almost as many men as commerce and industry together; in the year 1895 the number of its
employees was less by almost 2,000,000 than those of
industry alone. In thirteen years a complete change
of conditions had eventuated.

INDUSTRY AND AGRICULTURE.

The economic legislation of the Empire had to take
into account two possibilities of this fundamental
change. It might have given all its support to industry and commerce, anyway, favoured by circumstances and developing with strength and ease; it

might have strengthened what seemed strongest, have led Germany towards a transformation into a purely commercial and industrial State, and have left German agriculture to its fate.   Count Caprivi and his colleagues thought they ought to pursue this course. On the other hand, compensation for unfavourable circumstances might be given to agriculture by means of legislation, and the transformation of Germany into a one-sided industrial State might be opposed, and agriculture might be maintained, strong and vigorous, side by side with flourishing industry.

I embarked on this latter course with full knowledge of what I was doing, and with absolute conviction, when I introduced the Tariff Laws of 1902; for I was persuaded that vigorous agriculture is necessary for us from the economic but, above all, from the national and social points of view, just because the industrialisation of Germany continues to progress steadily.

I have always been of opinion that more can be learnt from personal intercourse and from life than from books, however profound.   I incline to think that one learns most in conversation with people holding different views which they know how to defend. "Du choc des opinions jaillit la vérité."   When, years ago,

I conversed with a Liberal of the Left about economic problems, I asked him at last: "And do you
think that at a pinch, if there were a terrible war or a
serious revolution, even with all their gifts and their
capabilities, and, of course, with a full claim to the
same treatment, commerce and industry, our splendid
new classes can, in the hour of danger, completely
take the place of those forces which made Prussia
great?" My political antagonist and personal
friend considered for a short time and then said:
"You are right; preserve our agriculture for us, and
even the Prussian nobility."

We owe much to industry and commerce. They
have made our land wealthy, and enable us, above
all, financially to support our armaments on land and
at sea. A distinguished man in German economic
circles, Prince Guido Henckel, used to say agriculture
must provide our soldiers and industry must pay for
them.

Industry and commerce, these two new lines of
business, feed and employ the great increase in our
population, which we lost formerly by emigration.
We rose to the height of a World Power on the shoul-
ders of commerce and industry. But the gains of
our national development in one direction have often

been paid for by losses in the other. To estimate the
real profit of German industrialisation, the losses and
damage caused by it must be included in the calcula-
tion. It is soon seen, then, that the course of modern
economic life imposes other and harder duties on us
than the task of continually forcing on with all our
might the growth of commerce and industry. Modern development has great dangers for national life,
and only if we succeeded in removing these could we
rejoice with a clear conscience in the new achievements. We had to proceed like a clever doctor, who
takes care to maintain all the parts and functions of
the body in a strong and healthy condition, and who
takes measures in good time if he sees that the ex-
cessive development of one single organ weakens the
others. German industry, as a matter of fact, grew
strong at the expense of agriculture during the first
decade of its development. If nothing were done,
agriculture threatened to fall under the hammers of
industry and be crushed. But that did not mean an
injury to agriculture alone; it meant, too, a loss for
the nation. Our agricultural forces that react on our
national life are too valuable and too indispensable
for us ever to be able to cease from caring with all
our might for the weal or woe of German agriculture.

The economic life of a nation is not like a business house with many branches, and to which these various branches are of more or less interest according to their chances of profit at the time.

HEALTH AND WEALTH OF THE NATION.

Apart from the fact that agriculture as a producer and as a consumer stands on a level of absolute equality with industry, other than purely economic points of view must be considered in estimating the economic strength of a nation. The political economy of a nation has not only an economic but also a national significance. It is not merely a question of the material gain due to the different kinds of work. It also depends on how the various occupations react on the maintenance and growth of the physical and ideal forces of the nation. Certainly a nation stands in need of increasing its wealth, its financial power to live. States in our days need this more than in former times. Modern government, with its enormous sphere of action, and, above all, modern armaments, demand very different material means than was the case formerly. But by material means alone a nation can neither maintain its place in the world nor advance it. Physical, moral and mental health are still the greatest national riches.

Prussia proved gloriously in the Seven Years' War and in the War of Liberation what a nation, poor but healthy in body and mind, can achieve; whereas superior wealth has never been able to prevent the disastrous consequences of diminishing strength in a nation.

A State is not a commercial company. In the rivalry of the nations of the earth industrial strength is of very considerable importance, but great and decisive events ultimately depend on quite other forces, and are not fought out in the field of industry. The truism, that wealth alone does not bring happiness, applies to nations as much as to individuals. Nations also can only enjoy increased wealth if they have a sound mind in a sound body. The Government, in its economic decisions, must not, like a clever speculative merchant, shape its course according to favourable circumstances which offer a brilliant prospect to one sphere of industry or another; it must subordinate its economic policy to national policy as a whole, must act so that not only the present industrial welfare of the nation is increased, but that, above all, the future sound development of the nation is ensured.

The question which political economy has often asked itself: "How does a nation get rich, so as to be able to live well?" must be supplemented for economic policy by the other question: "How does a nation keep healthy, so as to be able to live long?" Industry and commerce increase our national wealth to a greater degree and with greater speed than agriculture was ever able to do. But, without great and flourishing agriculture by its side, industry would soon use up the best forces of the nation, and would never be able to replace them. Agriculture is the mother of the nation's strength which industry employs, the broad acres in which the trees of industry and commerce stand, and from which they derive their nourishment.

We rightly admire in the industrial centres of the Rhineland, Westphalia and Saxony the keenness, the energy and the organising talent of the employers. In the perfection of the industrial machinery we admire the powers of invention and the audacity of our technical men and engineers. We find cause for admiration, too, in the quality of the industrial products, due to the diligence and conscientiousness of the German workman. We are rightly proud of the flourishing state of our great and middle-sized towns, which owe their quick development to the rise of industry and commerce.

Since the end of the Middle Ages we had experienced no development of cities on a large scale. And it is not fair to condemn the culture of the modern large towns without qualification, for, as in the Middle Ages, the many greater and more populous cities of modern times are centres of intellectual and artistic life. Among the influences which emanate from the large towns and penetrate into the country there are certainly some that have a pernicious effect on the habits of life of the country. But these injuries are often counterbalanced by the renewal and the refinement, of external culture which nowadays, as always, originate in the large towns. He who is not blind to the great dangers of an exaggerated development of the towns in our country must appreciate the very considerable achievements of our great cities in the spheres of intellect and culture, and must separate the wheat from the chaff.

It is not right either to seek the defects of our highly developed great towns too exclusively in the ethical domain. There is sin *intra* and *extra muros*. The just and the unjust are to be found in the country as well as in the towns. We must also not forget that particularly in the sphere of charity the towns have led the way with model institutions, and that in making provision for the lower classes the great employers of labour have done pioneer work.

The dangers of the industrialisation and the consequent "townification" of Germany do not lie so much in the spheres of intellect and moral life, so difficult to gauge and to estimate, but in the physical conditions. The health of the men and the fertility of the women suffer greatly under the influence of life in towns, and especially in large towns. For the years 1876–80 in the kingdom of Prussia the yearly average of living children born to women up to the age of forty-five was 160 per thousand in the towns and 182 per thousand in the country. For the years 1906–10 the numbers had fallen to 117 in the towns and 168 in the country. That means a loss of forty-three births per thousand women in the towns. In the municipal district of Berlin alone the numbers had fallen in the same space of time from 149 to 84, a loss of sixty-five. The rapid increase in the town populations does not connote an increase in the national population, but a steady decrease, for the women who migrate from the country to the towns, and the women who grow up in the towns effect a decrease in the birth-rate of the Empire. It is the same with the health of the men, as tested by their fitness

for military service.   According to the statistics com-
piled on the basis of the inquiry made by a Commission which I appointed in 1906, the country districts,
i.e. communities of less than 2,000 inhabitants, furnished 114 men who passed the military test, the big
towns of more than 100,000 inhabitants 65, the middle-sized towns of 20,000 to 100,000 inhabitants 83
per 100 men due as calculated on the basis of the total
population.   Of the parents of those fit for service,
74.97 per cent. came from the country, 1.68 per cent.
from the large towns.   And Germany has forty-eight
towns with more than 100,000 inhabitants, France
only fifteen, Italy thirteen, Austro-Hungary nine.
Almost two-thirds of our population live in the towns
and industrial centres.   In the year 1850 agriculture
employed 65 per cent.; in 1870, 47 per cent.; in 1899,
32 per cent.; and in 1912 only 28.6 per cent. of the
total population.

These figures are of very serious import.   They
show that every weakening of agriculture means a
weakening of our power of defence, a diminution in
our national strength and safety.   Commerce and industry have only flourished so because peace was preserved by the strength of our armaments, and they
will only be able to continue to thrive in the future

if the protection of our armaments is maintained in undiminished strength. That, however, demands a strong and numerous rural population, who can find in highly developed agricultural industry sufficient work to earn their livelihood. Commerce and industry for their own sake must be deeply interested in the prosperity of agriculture. As the statistics show, in future even more than was the case since the end of the 'nineties, the task of protecting trade and property in the Empire will fall to the rural population.

THE PROTECTION OF AGRICULTURE.

A Liberal savant, an old friend of mine, said to me some years ago in Norderney, as he watched the ships which passed my house, that he could not understand how I, otherwise a sensible man, could have given our industrial policy such an agrarian tendency by means of the tariff. I pointed to a ship that was just passing, and said: "A ship without sufficient ballast, with too high a mast, and too heavily rigged, will turn turtle. Agriculture is our ballast. Commerce and industry are to be our mast and sails. The ship cannot advance without them. But without ballast it will capsize." The captain of a ship must certainly try to make good headway. But he must not acquire speed at the expense of safety. If the ship of our Empire is to pursue her proud course with speed and safety, then the navigators must see that agriculture weighs heavy in the hull of the ship.

The protection of agriculture is a national duty of great importance—a duty which would have to be fulfilled, even if agriculture were of far less economic value than is actually the case. Although agriculture no longer occupies the paramount position in industrial life that it did formerly, yet it holds its own among the other branches of trade. It is true that according to the census of 1907 only 17,680,000 inhabitants are occupied in agriculture as opposed to nearly 26,380,000 in industry; but the value of its produce is equal to that of the produce of industry, or even surpasses it. Statistics on the subject do not supply sufficient data, and therefore the question whether agriculture or industry is more profitable cannot be answered definitely in favour of one or the other. Many a townsman, however, will be surprised to learn that the yield of one agricultural product alone, namely, milk, was 2,600 million marks in the year 1906, while the yield of all the mines in the same year only amounted to 1,600 million marks. The estimates formed by agriculturists and by industrialists as to the total value of agricultural and industrial products are not in agreement.

But whether, as regards the yield, agriculture or industry stands first, that is really of little or no importance; we need them both, and the downfall of one could never find full compensation in the rise of the other. To estimate the real economic value of the products it would be necessary to ascertain also in what manner agriculture and industry react on the stimulation and on the money-making powers of commerce. And even then one would still have to take into consideration that the value of the yield is influenced by the fluctuation of prices in the world's markets. These questions are of more interest from the point of view of the scientific investigation of economic life than from that of the practical political treatment of economic forces.

FOREIGN AND HOME MARKETS.

Industrial goods are disposed of in the foreign market, on the Continent and overseas, and in the home market in Germany itself. The development of our railway systems, our natural waterways, our canals, and the oversea traffic growing ever greater under the protection of the German navy, have brought the foreign market within easier reach. Industry has need of the foreign market in order to maintain its present development, to extend it and to provide millions of workmen with sufficiently profitable work.

For this reason it is the duty of economic policy to conclude favourable commercial treaties of long duration in order to keep the foreign market open. But, all the same, the home market is also of very great importance. It would be called upon to replace the foreign market if in time of war our national frontiers should wholly or partly be closed. But in the home market, agriculture is by far the most important customer of industry; only if agriculture is able to buy, if it earns enough itself to enable others to earn too, will it be able, in critical times, to consume a part of the products which cannot be disposed of abroad. The old proverb, "If the peasant has money then everyone else has too," is literally true, as soon as industry is forced, to a greater extent than is necessary in times of peace, to find its customers at home.

A policy which only considers the demands, moods and chances of the moment, which only does that which at the time is easiest to do, which only works *ad hoc,* without thought for future results, cannot claim any merit. Not even the best considered policy can include every future contingency in its calculations.

But every one of our actions and of our decisions is the cause of future effects, and it may well be expected of a statesman that he foresee at least a part of the possible results of his policy.

Above all there are certain contingencies which must be reckoned with, because they have occurred again and again, at greater or lesser intervals, in the past, and come under the category of indestructible elements of the world's history. War is such a contingency and must be reckoned with in every statesman's calculations. No sensible man desires it. Every conscientious Government seeks to avoid it so long as the honour and vital interests of the nation permit of so doing. But every State department should be organised as if war were going to break out to-morrow. This applies to economic policy as well.

THE IMPORTANCE OF AGRICULTURE IN TIME OF WAR.

Owing to the sense of security induced by a long period of peaceful prosperity, we are more inclined than is good for us, to make our arrangements with regard to economic matters as if this peace would be permanent. Even if we had not been threatened with war during the last decades we must realise that there is no such thing as permanent peace, and must remember Moltke's words: "Permanent peace is a dream, and not even a beautiful one. But war is an essential element of God's scheme of the world."

There is no part of public or private life that would be untouched by war. But the effects of war are most directly felt and most palpable in economic matters. The results of a war, be it successful or unsuccessful, put in the shade the results of even the most serious economic crisis. Economic policy must foster peaceful development; but it must keep in view the possibility of war, and, for this reason above all, must be agrarian in the best sense of the word.

As in time of war, industry is dependent on the buying power of agriculture, the productive power of agriculture is a vital question for the whole nation. There are parties and groups representing certain economic interests which demand that the Government shall place a very small duty on agricultural products from abroad, particularly the most important, corn and meat, or even let them in duty free, so that the price of comestibles, under the pressure of foreign competition, may be kept low, and thus the

industrial workman's expenses of living may be reduced. They want to base all economic policy on an
imaginary permanent peace. Our agriculture, which
has to compete, so far as wages are concerned, with
the high wages paid by industrial concerns, which has
to employ the most modern and expensive machinery
in order to pursue intensive culture on soil that has
been tilled for centuries, is absolutely unable to produce at the same price as the large, young agricultural
countries, which work virgin soil and pay small wages.

Our agriculture needs a protective tariff. Imported agricultural products must have a sufficiently
heavy duty imposed on them to prevent the foreign
supply from falling below a price at which our home
agriculture can make a fair profit. The reduction
of agrarian duties at the time of Caprivi's commercial policy, brought about a crisis in our agriculture
which it was only able to weather by dint of working
with stubborn energy, and hoping for a complete
change of tariff arrangements within a short time.
If we sacrificed the protective tariff on agricultural
products in order to lower the cost of living by means
of cheap imports, the danger would arise that agricultural work would grow more and more unprofitable,
and would have to be given up to a greater and greater

extent. We should go the way England has gone.

During the time when there were strained relations between Germany and England, I once explained to an English statesman how utterly unfounded and even nonsensical was the English fear of a German attack, let alone a German invasion. Whereupon he replied: "All you say is right, and, so far as I am personally concerned, you tell me nothing new. But with regard to English public opinion and the man in the street, you must not forget that England's position is very different from that of the Continental Powers. France suffered a terrible defeat, but a few years after Gravelotte and Sedan she had recovered so far that it was possible to contemplate 'war in sight.' Almost as quickly Austria got over the effects of 1859 and 1866. After the Japanese War, in spite of serious defeats on land and at sea, and of a grave revolution, Russia's favour did not cease to be courted on more than one side. England is different. Eighty per cent. of our population lives in cities. Our agriculture is unable to produce more than a fifth of the wheat and a half of the meat consumed in England. If our navy were defeated, and England were cut off from foreign trade, within a very few weeks we should be reduced to the choice between starvation and anarchy on the one hand and an unconditional peace on the other." Countries where agriculture flourishes, countries where at least a great part of the population is engaged in tilling the soil, where agriculture supplies the home market in part, and provides a large portion of the necessary foodstuffs, have greater powers of resistance in critical times, and recover far more easily after such, than countries that are dependent entirely on commerce and industry. Carthage experienced that as opposed to Rome. Even the highest industrial wages are of no avail if the workman can buy no food in the country with his money.

And this state of affairs can arise if, in time of war, the frontiers are wholly or largely closed, and home agriculture is not in a position to provide a sufficient amount of foodstuffs. What we might gain in peace, and for the moment, by surrendering our agriculture to foreign competition, we might ultimately have to pay for in war with misery, hunger and their fatal consequences to the State and society. Our agriculture can only maintain numerous and, above all, productive undertakings if it is protected by a sufficient duty on imported agricultural produce. This protection it must receive.

JUSTICE TOWARDS ALL THE WORKING CLASSES.

It is the duty of the State to look after the welfare of all classes of workers and the people in general. It must not allow an industry of economic importance, like agriculture, which is indispensable to the nation, to suffer in order that other branches of industry may thrive the more easily and quickly. The State must grant its aid in proportion to individual needs, and must make the nation in general share the necessary burdens. As it is right that the working classes should receive direct grants from the Imperial exchequer, so it is right that the existence of agriculture should be indirectly assured by means of the tariff. Both are a *nobile officium* of the State. It is just as misleading to speak of favouritism in regard to agriculture because of the policy of protective duties, as it is to speak of favouritism towards the working classes because of our social policy. True justice on the part of the State does not lie in granting or refusing the same thing to each class, each trade, or each citizen, so that there may be no external differences; that would only be mechanical justice. Real justice lies in giving to each, as far as is possible, what he most needs. This is the justice I

meant when, two months before the introduction of
the Tariff Bill, at a dinner on September 21, 1901,
given me at Flottbeck, my birthplace, by the provincial diet of Pinneberg, I defined the economic policy
of His Majesty's Government as one that desired to
give to each what he required, true to the old motto
of the Hohenzollern, *"Suum cuique."* Our tariff
policy has to fulfil a double purpose. It must, on
the one hand, by means of sufficient protection, maintain home products in agriculture and industry in a
position to compete with foreign goods. On the other
hand, by means of commercial treaties of long duration, it must keep the foreign markets open to our industrial exports and foreign trade. In order to accomplish this first task we must surround ourselves
with a barrier of duties; in order to do justice to the
second we must arrange our protective tariff in such
a way as not to make it impossible for other countries
to conclude commercial treaties with us on terms which
are more or less acceptable to them. Commercial
treaties are like mercantile business contracts. Both
parties ask more than they expect to get ultimately,
and gradually reduce their demands, until, on the
basis of some middle course, the business is concluded.
Both parties try to obtain the greatest possible ad-

vantages at the smallest possible cost. The salient point for the State is this, to see that no important economic interests are sacrificed. A middle course must be found between protective tariffs and commercial policy by means of which agriculture, commerce and industry can progress equably and side by side.

THE CAPRIVI-MARSCHALL TARIFF POLICY.

Owing to a momentary standstill in exports the Caprivi-Marschall Tariff Policy was directed entirely towards commercial treaties. In order to be able to conclude favourable commercial treaties as easily and rapidly as possible, foreign countries were offered a reduction in the duty on corn. But the opinion of clever business men, that the demands of the other parties increase in proportion as they are offered more, proved to be right in the end. The important commercial treaty with Russia, who derived great advantages from the reduction in the duties on cereals, was only concluded after negotiations which lasted three full years and were interrupted by a tariff war. Agriculture had to pay for the commercial treaties, since it had for the space of twelve years to work under considerably less favourable conditions, owing to the reduction in the corn tax from five to $3\frac{1}{2}$ marks. That was, as Bismarck expressed it at the time, a leap in the dark. The commercial treaties themselves, of course, had a very stimulating effect on trade. But this was at the expense of a great industrial class, indissolubly bound up with the economic welfare of the whole nation and with our great national traditions; this class, feeling slighted, fell into a condition of violent unrest and excitement.

It cannot be denied that, owing to an economic policy that, by injuring one class of industry, favoured the others, the economic differences in the nation were intensified. Up to the beginning of the 'nineties agriculture had on the whole advanced hand in hand with the other industries. Now it assumed a defensive position, formed the Association of Farmers in 1893, a very strong organisation which, in common with all societies representing economic interests, gradually grew more and more intemperate in its attitude and demands. The belief that commerce and export industries gain, if agriculture loses, has its origin in the early 'nineties. This mistake introduced a factor of dissension and unrest into our home politics, which has often acted in a disturbing manner, calculated to hinder development.

THE TARIFF POLICY OF **1902** AND ITS OPPONENTS.

It was the task of the new century to find a just compromise in economic policy, in the interests of agriculture.　This was necessary, not only for reasons of State justice, but, above all, because it became clear that the belief that agriculture could prosper in spite of the tariff reductions had not been justified.　Therefore, in the year 1901, I introduced the new Tariff Bill, on the basis of which new commercial treaties were to be concluded which should consider the legitimate interests of agriculture.　By placing our commercial policy on an agrarian foundation, we gave added strength to the economic life of the nation.　But the change to agrarian policy must not be accomplished in such a way as to be a hindrance or, what would be worse, a set-back to the development of commerce; i.e. the new tariff must make it possible to conclude favourable commercial treaties of long duration.

The "middle course" that I gave out as a watchword before the tariff fight, was thus clearly indicated. If the whole matter was not to come to grief it was necessary to be moderate on the agrarian side as well. In the preamble to the Government's Bill it was said:

"Germany's future commercial policy will have to be founded on the principle that measures in favour of export industry must not lead to a reduction in the protective duties which are indispensable to agriculture. On the other hand, export industries will be entitled to expect that consideration of agriculture, at their expense, shall not go beyond what is absolutely needful." This problem was set us by the tariff laws, and in the course of long parliamentary battles, fought with almost unexampled obduracy, it was solved.

As soon as the new tariff rates were made known, the Free Trade Press declared that it would be impossible to conclude commercial treaties on the basis of this new tariff: the end of German commercial policy was said to be at hand. The extreme Agrarian papers were of the opinion, on their part, that the tariff would not satisfy even the most unpretentious farmers. The Socialist Press said: "Down with the extortionate tariff." The Government was attacked on both flanks and had to break in the middle in order to carry its work which was in the interests of the whole community and especially of agriculture, to a successful finish.

If two extreme views or demands are opposed to

each other, then, in politics as in life, common sense and truth usually lie midway between them. Free trade democracy demanded that agriculture should be sacrificed to commercial policy. The Association of Farmers demanded that the prospect of commercial treaties should be sacrificed to agrarian policy. One was as impossible as the other. Agrarian opposition, as well as free trade opposition, had to be overcome. The attack from both sides was very violent. Only if the Government remained inflexible on the main points, if it did not allow itself to be dragged over by the opposition on the Right or on the Left, could it hope to see the parties, when they had moderated their demands, agree to the middle course which it had planned. The Social Democrats and Ultra-Liberal Association resorted to obstruction in order to make discussion of the clauses of the Bill impossible, and so force a General Election. With praiseworthy impartiality the deputy, Eugen Richter, although he and his party friends were not in favour of the tariff proposals, protested in the name of the Ultra-Liberal People's party against this violence offered to the majority by the obstruction of the minority.

For a time it seemed as if it would be impossible to

get a majority for the Tariff Bill, as part of the Right, on the principle of "everything or nothing," seemed inclined to refuse the whole tariff reform, undertaken in the interests of agriculture. It was greatly to the credit of the Chairman of the German Agricultural Council, Count Schwerin-Löwitz, of Count Kanitz, who unfortunately died in the prime of life, and, above all, of the leader of the Conservative party at that time, Count Limburg-Stirum, that they did not allow themselves to be overcome by the hyper-agrarian opposition, nor allow the Conservative party to embark on a wrong course. The deputy, Herr Bassermann, showed equally praiseworthy insight and power of resistance with regard to the free trade tendencies of a section of the Liberals. Thus Conservatives, National Liberals and the Centre led with statesmanlike ability by Count Ballestrem and the deputy, Herr Spahn, met on the ground of the motion proposed by the free Conservative deputy, Herr v. Kardorff.

The opposition of the Association of Farmers, which in other respects had done so much for the cause of agriculture, shows how the best cause is injured by excess. For the sake of unattainable advantages the realisation of possible ones was jeop-

ardised. The whole Tariff Bill, which was intended
to help agriculture out of the plight in which it had
so long been, was to be rejected because it did not
grant everything that was demanded. It has been
said that the opposition of the Association of Farmers
strengthened the position of the Government, both
with regard to Foreign Powers and with regard to
the parties, and thus contributed to ultimate success.
That is not correct. The Federal Governments had
left no doubt from the very first as to what they would
concede and what they would refuse. They had
stated clearly that they would make no fundamental
concessions, either on the one side or on the other. I
was sufficiently convinced of the necessity of greater
tariff protection for agriculture to withstand the attack from the Left. On the other hand it was obviously our duty not to block the prospect of soon
concluding new commercial treaties of sufficient duration, by tariff barriers which would have been insurmountable for foreign countries. The hyperagrarian
opposition did not strengthen the Government, but
it sharpened the weapons of the opposition. Economic differences were intensified, and in commercial circles and those of export industry the erroneous
idea gained ground, that between their interests and

those of agriculture there was a chasm that could not be bridged.

The belief of the extreme Agrarians, however, that immediately after the rejection of the Government's proposals another tariff would be introduced that would embody the tariff rates advocated by the Association of Farmers, was utterly and completely without foundation. The Federal Governments considered it absolutely necessary to continue the commercial policy, and looked upon this as an indispensable condition for any tariff. In the Federal Council no majority could have been found for a *va-banque* game in tariff policy, in which our whole economic policy would be staked on the one card of an extreme tariff. The rates of the Government's tariff represented the extreme limit to which the Federal Governments were willing to go.

If this tariff had been wrecked by Agrarian opposition, one of a more agrarian trend could not possibly have been introduced. The old Caprivi rates would have remained in force, and there the matter would have ended. Perhaps for a long time all would have remained unchanged. The *Kreuzzeitung* went too far when it said in those times of struggle that the Association of Farmers was shamefully leaving

its country in the lurch in the hour of need. But
it is a fact that the representatives of great economic
interests would have done much damage to those interests which they otherwise cared for so wisely and
energetically, had it not been for the firm attitude
of the Government and the wisdom of the Conservative leaders. This is a case which, unfortunately, is
not without parallel in the history of the home policy
of our country.

THE RESULTS OF THE TARIFF LAW OF 1902.

Thanks to the Tariff Law of 1902, our economic
policy regained that agrarian bias so indispensable to
the interests of the whole community. Side by side
with the foreign trade, advancing with such mighty
strides, the maintenance of a strong home industry
was secured. German agriculture, under the influence of the new tariff and of the commercial treaties
based on it, has experienced a decade of vigorous development. Our robust and hardworking farmers recovered the feeling that the Empire had an interest
in the success of their work; that it no longer looked
upon agriculture as an industrial stepchild, but as
one having equal rights and, indeed, as the first-born
of its mother Germania. The number of agricul-

tural undertakings increased by nearly 180,000 between 1895 and 1907. The amount of live stock increased enormously, cattle by about 3,000,000 head, pigs by about 5,300,000, in the same space of time. The harvest of rye in 1909 was 11,300,000 tons* as against 6,600,000 in 1895; wheat, 3,750,000 tons, as against 2,800,000; barley, 3,500,000 tons, as against 2,400,000; oats, 9,100,000 tons, as against 5,200,000; potatoes, 46,700,000 tons, as against 31,700,000.

In comparison with the agriculture of other countries, ours has developed quite extraordinarily in the last decade. In the summer of 1902, not long before the second debate on the tariff, the historian of German agriculture, Dr. Freiherr v. d. Goltz, had to conclude the opening remarks of his work with the statement that, "owing to events in the sphere of national and international economics, German agriculture was passing through a critical period." To-day, qualified judges of agricultural conditions point proudly to the flourishing development, the growing value of the yield and the increased power of production (which is capable of still further increase) of German agriculture.

* The German ton is not quite so much as the English, being equal to 2.205 lbs. avoirdupois.

But the agricultural development has not taken place at the cost of the expansion of our industrial export trade or of our commerce. The free trade prophets, who in the debates of 1901 and 1902 prophesied that the agrarian trend of our economic policy would "restrict commerce," have proved wrong. Those who believed that it would not be possible to conclude favourable commercial treaties of long duration, on account of the increased agrarian duties, had underestimated Germany's economic importance in the world. Germany, with the weapon of her new tariff in her hand, had by no means too little to offer other countries; in 1891 she had offered too much. When introducing the Caprivi-Marschall Tariff and Commercial Policy, the assumption had been made, amongst others, that the excess of our imports over our exports must force us to special concessions in order to open the foreign markets still further to us. As a matter of fact, the large amount of our imports, our ability to buy, was the strongest point in our position when concluding our commercial treaties. We could expect concessions because we are such excellent customers of foreign countries. We were able successfully to make use of the relation between our imports and our exports in the opposite sense to that employed at the beginning of the 'nineties.

The commercial treaty with Russia, round which a contest raged between 1891 and 1894, was concluded between Count Witte and myself with comparatively little difficulty in Norderney in July, 1904. The other commercial treaties followed, and in no case did the new tariff prove an insurmountable obstacle. Under the commercial treaties based on the tariff of 1902 commerce and industry have steadily continued their brilliant development.

The number of persons employed in commerce and industry is continually on the increase, as is the number of large undertakings. The rapid growth of general prosperity, chiefly due to industry and commerce, is quite obvious. To take one example from among many, the official statistics in the year 1909 report 4,579 commercial companies with a capital of 15,860 million marks, which pay yearly dividends to the amount of about 1,000 million. The large private banks have become a power, not only in the industrial world, but in the sphere of economic policy. German imports in general rose between 1903 and 1911 from 6,300 million marks to 10,300 million; exports, from 5,300 million to 8,700 million. And following the development of foreign trade, the German mercantile marine increased (in 1,000 gross registered tonnage) from 2,650 in 1900 to 4,267 in 1909, and 4,467 in 1911. In the German shipyards the construction of ships, including river craft and warships, rose from 385 in 1900 to 814 in 1909 and 859 in 1911. Since, at the same time, during the last decade, social provision has not only been further developed for the working classes, but has been extended to the middle classes, we may say that all classes engaged in trades and professions have maintained and developed their flourishing condition since our economic policy took an agrarian turn, while agriculture has been rescued from a critical condition, and has taken its place in the ranks of the general, thriving development of German industrial life.

From the economic point of view in particular the German nation has reason to be content with the result of their development during the last decade, and to hope that the courses on which they have embarked, and which have proved so profitable, will not be abandoned. The advantages gained by commerce and export through the inauguration of commercial policy at the beginning of the 'nineties have been maintained. The whole of German industry has been able uninterruptedly to enjoy the protection of the tariff granted in the year 1878. Individual defects of the Caprivi tariff were remedied in favour of industry by the tariff of 1902. Finally, German agriculture has acquired the necessary protective duties.

More has been done for the workmen in Germany than in any other country. When, a few years ago, a deputation of English trades unions made a circular tour through Germany, to study the conditions of our working classes, one of the Englishmen, after being made acquainted with our arrangements for the welfare of the working man, asked one of his German guides (a Social Democrat, by the way) in astonishment, "But what do you go on agitating for?"

ECONOMIC POLICY AND PARTY POLITICS.

If, in spite of everything, we have not achieved industrial peace, if the antagonism between different industrial classes continues to be violent, if on the contrary passion runs higher in the field of industry, and the quarrels and hatred between the various industrial classes are bitterer than ever, the cause does not lie in any defect or any lack of adjustment in our economic policy, but in the imperfection of our home politics.

Just as in purely political questions the German parties as a rule determine their attitude not by considerations of expediency, but by their hostility for the time being to one party or another, so they do to a far greater extent on questions of economic policy. Germany is probably the only country in which practical economic questions are weighed with scrupulous care in the party balance. With the single exception of the Centre, which is practical even in these matters, every party, great or small, has its own economic policy or, at least, its own specialty in economic policy to which economic questions are subordinated. That is part and parcel of party dogmatism. We have almost as many different conceptions of financial policy, agrarian policy, commercial policy, trade policy, social policy, tariff policy, rating policy and other kinds of economic policy, as we have parties. The German party man gets so wrapped up in the views of his party on economic questions that soon, by auto-suggestion, he comes to consider these views as indissolubly bound up with his own trade interests and his own livelihood, and, so far as economic matters are concerned, carries on party warfare with a violence that can only be inspired by selfishness. We have no party that can say that it represents one

single form of industry, not even the Social Democrats can assert that of themselves. Nevertheless,
with the exception of the Centre, every party has
often carried on the struggle in economic politics more
or less as if for each one it were a question of representing one particular interest. True, the Conservatives base their attitude chiefly on landed property,
the National Liberals on industry, and the Ultra-
Liberals on commerce. That is due to the political
traditions of the various classes. But if the parties
develop more and more into representatives of the
interests of special professions and trades, that will
involve great dangers with regard to economic, political and national questions.

If the different industrial classes confront each
other as so many political parties, it will no longer be
possible to dispose of questions of economic policy in
such a manner as to profit all branches of industry.
The different interests will become totally irreconcilable. Each class will see its own gain in the other's
loss. And the industrial differences will, if the Government is not in strong hands, be decided, like party
struggles for power, by beating the minority party
by a majority vote, with a total disregard of the interests of whole industrial classes.

On the other hand, professional and industrial classes are rarely capable of deciding great national questions independently, with a view to the position of the Empire in the world, instead of to their own professional interest. And they are the less capable of this the more a national task involves material sacrifices. An amalgamation of the ideas of party politics with those of an industrial class would constitute an equally great danger for national and for industrial life. Neither agriculture, nor commerce, nor industry, but the Social Democrats ultimately, would profit by this.

IV

THE EASTERN MARCHES

A DISTINCTION must be made between the domain of
State rule and a nation's ownership. The two rarely
coincide. The attempt to make them fit, whether it
be by obtaining State control over regions where the
nation has settled, or whether it be by spreading national civilisation in the domain where the State has
power, is responsible for a great number of complications in recent history. It has found its most modern
expression in that form of colonial policy which is
called, sometimes not quite rightly and sometimes
quite wrongly, Imperialism.

STATE AND NATIONAL OWNERSHIP.

Nations of military ability and economic skill and
of superior culture, will mostly reach further with
the arm of their State power than with the sway
of their national culture, and will expend their energy
on making the national conquest follow in the wake
of the political.

Weak and incapable nations must look on while

foreign nationalities gain in number and importance
within the borders of their State.

There is no third course. In the struggle between
nationalities one nation is the hammer and the other
the anvil; one is the victor and the other the van-
quished. If it were possible in this world to separate
nationalities definitely and clearly by means of frontier posts and boundary stones, as is done for States,
then the world's history and politics—by which history is made—would be relieved of their most difficult task. But State boundaries do not separate nationalities. If it were possible henceforward for members of different nationalities, with different language
and customs, and an intellectual life of a different
kind, to live side by side in one and the same State,
without succumbing to the temptation of each trying
to force his own nationality on the other, things on
earth would look a good deal more peaceful. But
it is a law of life and development in history, that
where two national civilisations meet they fight for
ascendancy.

In that part of old Poland where, after the partition, most was done to meet Polish wishes, it is perhaps shown more clearly than anywhere else that
where two nationalities are bound to the same spot,

it is very difficult to make both contented; that given such conditions, friction easily arises; and that it can happen that measures, adopted on the one side in good faith, may rouse excitement and opposition on the other. Did the Poles succeed in contenting the Ruthenians in Galicia? Do not the Ruthenians in the Carpathians and on the Pruth make the same complaints as the Poles on the Warthe and the Vistula, or even more violent ones?

Other countries, too, resound with the battles of nationalities, and the accusations of one nationality against another. Every nation is convinced of the higher value and consequently of the better right of its own civilisation, and is inspired by a strong desire, which is like an unconscious natural force, to attain more and more authority for its own civilisation. Not every nation is conscious of this force. The great Roman generals and statesmen were well aware of it, when they advanced, conquering as they went, into Greece, Asia Minor, North Africa, above all into Gaul and Germany where they followed up the conquest by arms, with the conquest by superior Roman civilisation.

Such a steady consciousness of national civilisation exists to-day among the English people. The Eng-

lishman is deeply imbued with the idea of the superiority of Anglo-Saxon culture. He certainly disap-
proves at times if other nations make more or less energetic propaganda for their own culture, but he seldom raises the question whether England might not
be justified in taking such proceedings herself. He
is convinced that English rule and the consequent
Anglicising is a blessing, and he bases his right to expansion and conquest on his sense of the superiority
of Anglo-Saxon civilisation and Anglo-Saxon institutions. The grand fabric of the British Empire,
the greatest the world has seen since the Roman Empire, for which no sacrifice of life or property was
ever refused, was and is supported by the steadfast
consciousness and firm intention on the part of Eng-
glish people of being bearers of a higher civilisation
to every spot where English power extends. The
English belief in the superiority of their own intellectual, moral, religious, legal and economic life is
the vital force in English national policy.

Higher civilisation has always bestowed political
rights. The belief in a real or supposed higher civilisation has always provoked a claim to rights.
When France, after the Great Revolution, flooded
Europe with her armies, she based her right to con-

quest on the supposed blessings of Republican freedom.   She felt herself the bearer of superior political culture to other nations, especially the Germans
and Italians.   In our country in particular there were
not a few who recognised this right, and were only
cured of their error by the bitter experiences of Napoleonic despotism.   The civilising mission of the
French Revolution was based on a fundamental mis-
conception of the nature of civilisation in which, compared with religion, morals, law and education, political institutions have a subordinate value, and it con-
demned itself by the growing brutality of Napoleonic
rule.   But there are civilising missions which are justified.   For instance, those that the Christian Colonial
Powers have to fulfil in Africa at the present time.
Thus Russia is justified as a bearer of higher civilisation to Asia.   And if ever the battle between the
higher and lower civilisation should cease in the
world's history, our belief in the further development
of mankind would lose its foundation.   We should
be bereft of a great and ideal hope.

THE WORK OF COLONISATION IN THE EAST OF GERMANY.

It was a mission of civilisation that in the past led
us Germans across the Elbe and the Oder towards the

East. The work of colonisation in the east of Germany, which, begun nearly a thousand years ago, is not yet concluded to-day, is not only the greatest but the only one in which we Germans have succeeded. Never in the history of the world was less blood spilt or less violence used in colonising on such a large scale as this. This is particularly true of German colonisation in what was formerly Poland. For centuries the German colonists, often summoned to the country by its kings, lived as loyal Polish subjects and taught the Poles higher civilisation. Even those times, when the Germans were oppressed in Poland and often deprived of their rights, tell no story of German revolt there. When the Poles proved themselves unfit to maintain government, and the strong Prussian State with its law and order assumed control of parts which had formerly belonged to the domain of Poland, the work of German civilisation had been going on in these parts for centuries already. The rare case supervened that the establishment of State rule followed and did not precede the tasks of colonising and civilising. The annexation by the Prussian State of our Eastern provinces, Posen and West Prussia, would not and could not have come to pass if the Polish Republic of Nobles had been a

State capable of continued existence. When the in-
corporation in the German dominion of the Prussian
State took place, its effect was that of a belated, political requisition of rights which the German inhabitants
of West Prussia and Posen had created long before
by their civilising achievements. Quite apart from
the fact that if Prussia had not placed the Germans
in Poland under German rule, they would have fallen
under the dominion of Russia.

Our eastern provinces are our German new country. Although they were incorporated several generations earlier than Alsace-Lorraine and Schleswig-
Holstein, yet they are younger national acquisitions.
For one thing, in the West it is only old German domain that has been recovered, possessions where the
German Emperors held undisputed sway, before ever
a German had crossed swords with a Wend east of
the Elbe, or a German plough had furrowed Wendic
soil. This new land in the East, entered by right of
conquest at the time when Germany's Imperial power
was at its zenith, had to afford us compensation, from
the point of view of the State and above all of the nation, for losses of old possessions in the West.
"There was a time," I said in January, 1902, in the
Prussian Chamber of Deputies, "when one had to

speak with bated breath of the Holy German Empire, when the German Empire extended farther in the South and West than now. We do not dream of wishing that those times would return; we do not dream of extending our frontiers in any direction whatever. But what Providence has granted us as a compensation for our losses elsewhere, our possessions in the East, those we must and will retain."

Considered from a distance, the German movement from east to west, and then again to the east, appears as a uniform whole. In the seventh century we Germans abandoned all land east of the Elbe and penetrated far into the West, into the heart of France. Holland, Flanders, Brabant, Burgundy, Luxemburg and Switzerland were under the sway of the German Empire, were in part national German land. In the fourteenth century the upper course of the Rhone was the boundary of the German Empire. But these domains were lost, politically owing to the downfall of German Imperial power, nationally because our body as a nation was really not big enough to fill the wide garment of the Holy Empire. No sensible man will ever entertain the idea of recovering either national or political influence over the lands in the South and West which were lost so many centuries ago. At the time when we were losing ground in the West we had already found compensation in the East; the Germans were already streaming back into their old Germanic home which had been abandoned at the time of the so-called *Völkerwanderung* (migration of the nations), and into which Slavonic tribes had made their way. And the German colonists who settled east of the Elbe, beyond the Oder, on the banks of the Vistula and the Pregel, came from the Western territories; not a few from the very domains which we lost later on. It may well be said that a wave of the German nation flowed back again.

The great work of Eastern colonisation is the best and most permanent result of our brilliant history during the Middle Ages, a piece of work performed, not by a single German tribe, but by all of them together. One and all—Saxons, Franks, Bavarians, Suabians, Thuringians, Lorrainese, Flemish and Frisians—sent men of their tribe to the East of Germany—laymen and churchmen, knights and peasants. The new colony east of the Elbe at that time served to bridge the differences between the German tribes, which in some cases were very profound. It was common German land, with a population which has nothing and wished to be nothing but German, in contradistinction to the Wends and the Poles.

If, later on, it was the men from this mother-country of the Brandenburg-Prussian monarchy east of the Elbe, who in the hour of need manifested their will as Germans against the foreigner, if in our times it was by their means that under the black-and-white banner of the State of the German Order of Knight-hood the union of the German lands and German peoples in one Empire was realised, the first seeds were sown by the formation and settlement of these German colonies. For what they gave to the less hospitable East in the Middle Ages, the German tribes of the West and the South were repaid a thousand-fold by the East when Prussia brought State union to the whole of Germany.

The centuries of the Ottos, the Salic kings and the Hohenstauffens can show deeds and events of more dazzling brilliancy than the brave and diligent colonisation of the land east of the Elbe, but they can show nothing greater. The conquest of the old Prussian land by the German Order of Knighthood was but a pale reflection of the romantic glamour of the crusades and the expeditions to Rome. And the tough work of civilisation carried on by the monks in the eastern forests and marshes, and by the German citizens in the new and growing towns of the east, appears utterly prosaic and humdrum in comparison with the grand but unfortunate ventures of the world-policy of the old emperors. But, as so often in history, the brilliant achievements that drew all eyes, were for the moment only, soon to disappear; while the insignificant events which were accomplished on what was comparatively a side track of German history were the real things that were to be of value subsequently. To-day we think with more gratitude of the German Order of Knighthood that gave Prussia to us, of the Guelphs who won Holstein and Mecklenburg for us, and of the Ascanians of Brandenburg, than of the victories in Italy and Palestine. The most portentous national disaster was not the sad downfall of the Hohenstauffens owing to the intrigues of Papal and French policy, but the defeat of Tannenberg, which resulted in the loss of a large portion of the colonisation work of centuries, and the cession to the Poles of West Prussia and Danzig, and which put an end to the proud independence of the State of the German Order of Knighthood.

It was the wise statesmanship of the Hohenzollern electors that prevented our national possessions in the extreme east from slipping completely out of our grasp, and that here in the eastern outposts of Germany combined the interests of the German nation as a whole with those of the State of Brandenburg-Prussia. It may be questioned whether, had it not been for the black day of Tannenberg, the State of the Order of Knighthood would have been able to keep the East permanently German, in defiance of the superior power of Poland. There is no question but that we should have lost East and West Prussia for ever, as we had lost our western and southern domains in former times, if the House of Hohenzollern had not arisen as a tireless and cautious, but brave and determined, warden of the German Marches. The Great Elector asserted his rights to East Prussia—rights acquired by a clever family policy—at the point of the sword, when he bore the Red Eagle of Brandenburg to victory over the White Eagle of the King of Poland at the battle of Warsaw, and thus broke the bonds of Polish suzerainty. Very wisely the first King called himself King *in* Prussia, and thereby indicated the hope that his successors would be Kings *of* Prussia by ultimately acquiring West Prussia as well. And this hope was fulfilled when the Great King received West Prussia, at the first partition of Poland, as the prize of victory in the Seven Years' War, as Frederick the Great's biographer, Reinhold Koser, so well expressed it. Only to the victor of Rossbach, Leuthen and Zorndorf did the Empress Catherine grant a share of Polish land that had ceased to have any right to existence as a State since the Republic of Nobility had been in a condition of anarchy.

West Prussia was regarded, not as newly acquired foreign land, but as German land that had been recovered; and rightly so. For this country had become German, politically speaking, under the rule of the Order of Knighthood, and it had become German owing to the work of German settlers in town and country. But Prussia, besides giving back to the West Prussian Germans German rule and the glorious right to be German citizens of a German State, gave to her new Polish subjects freedom and rights.

King Stanislaus Leszczinski had lamented his country as the only one in which the mass of the people lacked all the rights of mankind. The mild yet stern, free yet limited, and just rule of the great Prussian King conferred on the Polish population what it had lacked before. "The surest means of giving this oppressed nation better ideas and morals will always be gradually to get them to intermarry with Germans, even if at first it is only two or three of them in every village," wrote Frederick the Great before the year of partition, 1772. Before a single foot of Polish land had come into the possession of the Germans the Great King, at a time when the nationality problem was still unknown, characterised Prussia's future task of civilisation as a Germanisation. Immediately after taking possession, he began the work of colonising, and sought and found settlers throughout Germany. The King, too, only continued what had been begun in the Middle Ages, the national conquest of the East of Germany, by means of settling German farmers in the country and German artisans, merchants and tradesmen in the towns. And when, in 1886, Bismarck proceeded to his policy of settlement on a larger scale, as in so many of his greatest national enterprises, he merely seized the reins that the Great King had held, and that had dragged along the ground since his death. A proof, amongst many others, how uniform is the national history of a people, and that from the national point of view there are not two possibilities of equal validity, but only one with a validity of its own.

Though it is true that in different circumstances we must not slavishly imitate the great models of the past, yet it is equally true that the great points of view by which our ablest men have been guided, maintain their worth for all times and on all occasions, and that they cannot be disregarded with impunity.

It is well known that of the huge addition of quondam Polish land which fell to Prussia's share at the second and third partitions of Poland, but little was left to her at the reconstitution in 1815—West Prussia and the present province of Posen, altogether not more than seven and a half per cent. of the old kingdom of Poland. Even though the province of Posen, with its Archbishopric dating from the year 1000, had become the heart of the Polish kingdom, yet in the course of centuries it had become that part of the great domain which was most strongly permeated with German elements. By incorporating this old-established German population in the eastern districts Prussia undertook a national German duty, in addition to her natural duties as a State towards the Poles who live within her borders and have become Prussian subjects.

Although the Poles have forfeited their right to independence, after being for centuries incapable of creating a strong State on the basis of law and order, none may shut their eyes to the tragic fate of this gifted and brave nation. Just as it is wrong in the necessary fight against the Social Democrats to hurt the feelings of the working classes, so it is wrong in the fight dictated by reasons of State against the propaganda for the re-establishment of a greater Poland, to hurt our Polish fellow-citizens who fought so bravely under the Prussian standards in the wars of 1866 and 1870. Because we prize our own nationality so highly we must respect the Pole and sympathise with the loyalty with which he clings to his national memories. But this respect and sympathy stop short of the point where the desire and ambition of the aforesaid propaganda begin, these being to jeopardise the Prussian monarchy and to attack its unity and solidarity. No consideration for the Polish people must hinder us from doing all we can to maintain and strengthen German nationality in the former Polish domains. Nobody dreams of wishing to thrust our Poles outside the borders of the Prussian Kingdom. Even the German opponents of a vigorous policy in the Eastern Marches admit how greatly the condition of the Poles has improved under Prussian administration; the Poles themselves cannot seriously deny it.

But it is the duty and the right of the Prussian Government to see that the Germans do not get driven out of the East of Germany by the Poles.

Nothing is further from the aims of our policy in the Eastern Marches than a fight against the Poles; its object is to protect, maintain and strengthen the German nationality among the Poles, consequently it is a fight for German nationality. This struggle, carried on with varying success and by various means, runs through the period of very nearly a century which has passed since the delimitation at the congress of Vienna of the boundaries of the re-established Prussian State. The task of solving this problem would probably have been easier for the Prussians and for the Poles if the artificial and untenable Grand Duchy of Warsaw, created by Napoleon, had not roused in the Poles the vain hope that in the course of European complications it might be possible to re-establish Polish independence. The Poles would very likely have been spared painful experiences on our side as well as on the other side of the frontier in 1830, 1848 and 1863, if the memory of the ephemeral creation of a State by the first Napoleon had not lived in their hearts. The thought that the partition of the Polish Republic among the Eastern Powers from 1793 to

1807 had only been temporary, naturally made it harder for the Poles, after the fall of Napoleon and the States he had founded to serve the military aims of France, to regard the accomplished facts as final.

PRUSSIA'S TASK.

The task Prussia had to fulfil in the domain, formerly Polish, that she had recovered in 1815 and that had been in her possession since 1772, was obvious enough. On the one hand, she had to oppose the propaganda for the re-establishment of Polish independence in a determined manner; on the other hand, she had to lavish great care on the maintenance and furtherance of German nationality in the eastern provinces. These two duties each involved the other, in so far as the national hopes of the Poles must lose ground in proportion as a strong contingent of Germans settled in the eastern provinces counterbalanced it.

If, at the beginning, after the War of Liberation, this task had been as clearly recognised and as firmly attacked as by Frederick the Great, the Prussian Government would not repeatedly in the course of temporary moods, which were misunderstood, have allowed itself to be diverted from the path so clearly indicated, and we should certainly have been considerably further on the road to the solution of our problem in the Eastern Marches. It has happened so often in politics that mistakes were made, not because with quick decision the obvious thing was done, but because, owing to sentiment and doubts, a clear and absolute decision could not be arrived at.

Even in politics the simplest thing, if not always, yet mostly is the best.

The expressions, "Conciliation Policy" and "Policy of Intrigue," with which the political opponents and supporters of a definite national policy in the Eastern Marches favour each other, characterise the various phases of our Prussian policy in Poland very superficially. The aim of Prussian policy in the Eastern Marches has always been to reconcile subjects of Polish nationality to the Prussian State and the German nation. There can be no doubt except as to the different means by which this reconciliation is to be attained. There has never been a question of anything else, whether it was Zerboni, the advisers of Frederick William IV., and Caprivi, or Flottwell, Grolmann, Bismarck, Miquel and I, myself, who determined the character of the policy in the Eastern Marches.

This policy must ultimately reconcile our Polish fellow-countrymen to the fact that they belong to the Prussian State and to the German Empire. Only this must not be achieved at the expense of our ownership in the East, or of the unity and sovereignty of the Prussian State.

It has rarely happened that a State has adopted such an unprejudiced and good-natured attitude towards members of another nationality living within its borders as Prussia adopted towards the Poles in the second and third decades of the nineteenth century. The blessings of the Stein-Hardenberg reforms were conferred on the Poles in full measure; an agricultural Loan Society helped Polish agriculture, which was in a terrible plight after the wars; a Provincial Diet in Posen ensured that local Polish interests should be represented; the members might be elected, and the people elected Poles; a Polish governor was associated with a Prussian president. The result was the revolt of 1830. Prussia had not only vainly striven to win the favour of the Poles. She had done more; for the sake of the Poles in the Eastern Marches she had forgotten to care for the Germans there, in that she had placed this German and Polish district under a purely Polish administration.

The men who worked in Posen from 1830–40, the President v. Flottwell and General v. Grolmann, bethought themselves once more of Prussia's duty in the East to men of German nationality. The second phase of our policy in the Eastern Marches began, which resumed the thread of the national traditions of the Middle Ages of the policy of the Great King, and which indicated the course of policy in the Eastern Marches to Bismarck and to me. The Polish Governor disappeared; by means of the suspension of elections for the Diet it became possible to appoint German officials, and, as far as the slender means of the Government permitted, a modest beginning was made to settle German landowners in the Eastern Marches. The policy of Flottwell was no more hostile to the Poles than was our later policy in the Eastern Marches, which continued on the lines he had laid down. In contradistinction to the unsuccessful policy of 1815–30, its only aim was to assist German nationality to its rights among the Poles, remembering the duties to Germans that Prussia had taken over when it gained possession of the old domain of the Colonists. In fact the Poles were deprived, not of their rights as citizens, but of privileges.

The attempt to reconcile the Poles to Prussian

government by granting them special rights was repeated in the decade following the transfer of Flottwell from Posen to Magdeburg, which took place in
1840; the culminating point was the so-called "national reorganisation" of Posen, which came to nothing. The "reorganisation" was to be effected in the
following way: the Eastern and more Polish part
of the province of Posen was to be separated from the
Western and more German part, and to be administered entirely by the Poles. The Poles demanded
complete autonomy in the whole province, like that
which Hungary now possesses in the Habsburg monarchy. The Germans in the province grew violently
excited at the threatened loss of their nationality.
The result of this unhappy attempt was a feeling of
hostility hitherto unknown between the two nationalities in the East.

After a long period in the 'sixties and 'seventies,
taken up with the work of founding and consolidating
the Empire, which resulted in indifference to the
struggle between the nationalities in the East, Bismarck in 1886 inaugurated his national policy in the
Eastern Marches on a large scale, after he had introduced State control of the schools in Posen in 1872,
and in 1873 the German language as that which was

to be used for instruction. The period of Flott-well's administration could be nothing but a correction in the national sense of the policy in the Eastern Marches. With Bismarck there began a determined fight for German nationality. Up till then the policy had been defensive, but, under Bismarck, Prussia began to take the offensive in order to rescue German nationality in the East, to maintain it and, if possible, to strengthen it. It is natural that the Poles were thrown into a state of violent excitement, that they prepared to defend themselves, and with their splendid organisation, largely supported by the Polish clergy, plunged into the fray. The antagonism between the two nationalities grew more acute. The policy pursued in the Eastern Marches influenced the whole of party politics, for the Centre supported its Polish co-religionists, and the Radicals thought it due to their principles to consider every step of the Prussian policy in the Eastern Marches as an exceptional measure which was contrary to their theoretical ideas of liberty. It is quite true that our home politics were not made easier by our national policy in the Eastern Marches, that a new cause of trouble and excitement was thereby added, and that the propaganda among the Poles in Prussia for the re-establishment of Polish independence grew more general and more violent.

The opponents of Prussian policy in the Eastern Marches, Germans as well as Poles, are fond of employing the argument that great unrest has been caused by this national policy, begun by Bismarck himself and carried on subsequently in accordance with his ideas. Such an argument can only bear upon the general political shell and not on the core of our national problem as regards the Poles. It means nothing more than the easy and cheap platitude, that in foreign as well as in home politics, peace and tranquillity may always be had if we strive to reach no goal which can only be attained with difficulty and by fighting. Such tranquillity is always pretty easy to get in politics.

The problem of our policy in the Eastern Marches is this: Shall we permit, shall we, by our inactivity, encourage the Eastern domains, i.e. Posen, West Prussia and certain parts of Upper Silesia and East Prussia, to slip once more from the grasp of German nationality, or not? Everyone who has national German feelings will answer that this must never happen, that it is the duty and the right of the Germans to maintain our national ownership in the East of Prussia, and, if possible, to increase it. The seventy years between the congress of Vienna and the inauguration of the Prussian policy of colonisation made it clear that neither scrupulous respect for Polish nationality, nor the ignoring of the nationality question in the East, could in the least prevent German nationality from being slowly but surely driven out of the East by that of the Poles. Only a well-thought-out scheme to further German nationality could prevent the latter from succumbing utterly. If the differences between the nationalities were thereby immediately intensified, it was certainly unfortunate, but it could not be avoided. In political life there are often hard necessities whose behests we obey with a heavy heart, but which must be obeyed in spite of sympathies and emotions. Politics is a rough trade in which sentimental souls rarely bring even a simple piece of work to a successful issue.

THE STRUGGLE FOR THE LAND.

With the fundamental Law of Settlement in 1886 Bismarck began the fight for the land on a big scale. He demanded and received a hundred million marks for the purpose of buying land and settling German peasants on it; that is, the purpose of increasing the numbers of the German element in the Eastern Marches. The work of colonisation is the backbone of Prussian policy in the Eastern Marches, for it settles Germans in the Eastern domain. And the whole problem in those parts is the problem of the relative numerical strength of the German population as compared with the Poles. The national acquirement of the eastern parts of Germany was begun by settlement a thousand years ago, and it is only by settlement that national possession can be maintained. The problem of the Eastern Marches is really not the least complex. Its solution depends less on political wisdom than on political courage.

Bismarck set to work vigorously on the basis of the new law, and during the first five years, from 1886 to 1890, about 46,000 hectares* were acquired from Polish owners. The beginning of the 'nineties afforded a splendid chance to the activities of the Settlement Commission, as an attendant phenomenon of an otherwise lamentable event. Owing to the plight of agriculture, the price of land fell rapidly, and it would have been easy to acquire a huge mass of land from Polish owners for the purposes of subsequent colonisation by Germans. But just at that time

* One hectare = 2.47 acres.

Count Caprivi thought it necessary, for parliamentary reasons, to propitiate the Poles. Concessions on the questions of schools and church were followed by assistance for the Polish Land Bank; that was equivalent to the rescue of the Polish landowners from whom the Settlement Commission had to endeavour to acquire land. The immediate and desired parliamentary object was in so far attained, that the Polish faction voted for the Army Bill of 1893.

But it soon became evident that the attitude of the parliamentary faction, as is often the case, did not correspond to the opinions of the party in the country. On the occasion of the discussion of the Navy Bill, the majority of the faction refused to follow their leader, Koscielski. Herr von Koscielski himself made that incautious speech at Lemberg in 1894, which contributed in a considerable degree to the change in Prussian policy in the Eastern Marches to the course laid down by Bismarck. At that time, in September, 1894, the German Association of the Eastern Marches was formed, after Germans from that district had visited the old Imperial Chancellor in Varzin and paid him homage.

The traditions of Bismarck found a prudent interpreter in Miquel after the retirement of Caprivi.

New funds were placed at the disposal of the Settlement Commission in 1898, and land was once more acquired on a larger scale. But the words of the poet, "Eternity will not bring back what one has refused to accept from a moment," again proved true in the case of our policy in the Eastern Marches. The favourable opportunity in the estate market, which had been allowed to slip at the beginning of the 'nineties, was past. The Polish landowners had been helped over the critical time; the Poles had had the chance of organising themselves for the battle for the land; whereas from 1886 to 1888 on an average 11,000 hectares were acquired yearly from the Poles by the Settlement Commission, it was only possible to buy from the Poles 911 hectares in 1895, 1804 hectares in 1896, and an average of 2,500 hectares yearly from 1897 to 1899. The land required for purposes of settlement had to be furnished more and more by German landowners.

The energy with which the Poles organised their resistance to the German attack on their soil deserves admiration. German activity in colonisation was replied to by Polish counter activity. The Poles, for their part, divided their estates into small lots, for which they found colonists to a great extent among the very numerous Polish industrial workmen in the West. While the Poles thought it shameful to sell land to the Germans, these latter unfortunately often did not object to selling German landed property to the Poles for a high price. I certainly succeeded, after replenishing the Settlement Fund in the year 1902, in furthering the work of colonisation to a very appreciable extent. Land for the purpose of settlement was acquired as follows: 22,007 hectares in the year 1902; 42,052 hectares in 1903; 33,108 hectares in 1904; 34,661 hectares in 1905; 29,671 hectares in 1906; and after a grant of fresh funds in 1908, 14,093 hectares in that year; 21,093 hectares in 1909.

But it grew more and more difficult to acquire estates from Polish landowners, as the Poles held fast to their land, and the activities of the Settlement Commission on the one hand, and the Polish policy of parcelling out their properties on the other, resulted in land speculation which sent up the price of estates enormously. If the work of colonisation, undertaken at such sacrifice and at the cost of such a hard struggle, was not to be doomed to ultimate failure, an idea had to be put into practice which Bismarck had expressed already in 1886, and which was discussed over and over again subsequently: the idea of disposses-

sion. The Dispossession Bill was the logical conclusion of the policy of colonisation begun in 1886; it
makes the Settlement Commission independent of the
variations of the estate market, and ensures ultimate
mastery to a strong Government in the economic
struggle for the land.

THE STRUGGLE FOR GERMAN CULTURE.

The struggle for the land, which in its essentials is
a struggle to permeate the eastern districts with a
sufficient number of Germans, will always be the
Alpha and Omega of our national German policy in
the East. This must be supported by the struggle
for German culture and education, and, above all, for
the German language. We certainly do not wish to
deprive the Pole of his mother tongue, but we must
try to bring it to pass that, by means of the German
language, he comes to understand the German spirit.
In our policy of settlement we fight for German nationality in the East; in our policy with regard to the
schools we are really fighting for Polish nationality
which we wish to incorporate in German intellectual
life. Here, again, we cannot proceed without severity, and this will increase or be mitigated as the Poles
increase or diminish their opposition. The founda-

tion of the German Technical Hochschule, or College, in the year 1904, and before that, of the Imperial Academy in Posen, in 1903, created, in the eastern districts, centres of German intellectual life which, let us hope, will gradually prove their powers of attracting students.

THE RESULTS OF THE POLICY IN THE EASTERN MARCHES.

Prussian policy in the Eastern Marches has never lacked violent critics, especially on the German side. The seemingly conclusive argument of these critics is the statement that our policy in the Eastern Marches has led to no palpable results, since after nearly twenty years of the policy of colonisation there is no appreciable change in the percentage of Germans and Poles in the population of the Eastern Marches. As an increase in the percentage of Germans was what Bismarck aimed at, our policy and, in particular, the work of colonisation must be considered to have failed. It is quite true that we have not nearly reached the goal of our policy in the Eastern Marches. Only if we pursue the course laid down by Frederick the Great, and later again adopted by Bismarck, not with small-minded chicanery, nor with

clumsy brutality, but with determination, and, above
all, consistently, can we hope, after a very considerable lapse of time, to fulfil our national task in the East
of Germany.

What we need most of all in our Eastern Marches
is steadfastness.   When I was visiting Posen in 1902,
the head of the Provincial Administration, v. Staudy,
for many years a Conservative member of the Reichstag, with whom I was staying, said to me at the conclusion of a long conversation about affairs in the
Eastern Marches: "And now one thing more: steadfastness! That is what everything depends on here.
Nothing has done us so much harm as our vacillation,
the fact that we gave in again and again. Now we
must hold out!"

The work of German colonisation in the Eastern
Marches, begun a thousand years ago, suspended for
four centuries, and taken up anew less than thirty
years ago, cannot be completed in a short time. This
is not like an ordinary political action, which is soon
followed by success or failure; we are in the midst of
a great historical evolution in which generation after
generation will have to co-operate. If from this
mighty point of view we regard our national work in
the East as a stage of evolution, then we may say

that success has not been denied us. In the years from 1886 to 1911, 394,398 hectares of land were acquired by the Government to provide for the settlement of German peasants; of these 112,116 hectares were formerly owned by Poles. On the settlement estates there are 150,000 Germans; 450 new villages have been built, and in 300 villages the number of Germans has been increased. The successes due to our policy of colonisation were convincingly stated by one of the most estimable statesmen of our time, Count Botho Eulenburg, in 1908, in the debate in the Upper Chamber on the Bill of Dispossession. As the last census shows, the decrease of the Germans as compared with the Poles has ceased, in spite of the higher birth-rate among the latter. These are results of palpable value, these are the first steady steps towards the still distant goal, which, however, can be attained, if we do not tire of this troublesome struggle entailing so many sacrifices, and if transitory phases of practical politics do not again sweep the great and permanent demands of national policy into the background.

We must also not deceive ourselves on the point that the German, in a struggle between nationalities, does not yet always possess the desirable power of resistance, and that only too often he runs the risk in such a struggle of losing his nationality, if the State does not protect and support him.   One of the chief difficulties of the problem in the Eastern Marches, and at the same time perhaps the strongest proof of the absolute necessity of a steadfast and strong policy there, lies in the need to strengthen the backbone of the German who, for reasons connected with our good and with our less good qualities, is so prone to be assimilated.   So far as this is concerned, the Government must take things as they are.   It is its duty to see that the Germans and their nationality do not succumb in the East.

However, the answer to the question as to what the state of affairs in the East of Germany would have been, had nothing been done for the protection and strengthening of German nationality there, affords a far better means of judging what has been accomplished than does an enumeration of positive achievements.   Before we can think of making national conquests in the East, our national possessions had to be protected from loss.   And we succeeded in so doing because we fought for them.   The development which Bismarck thwarted was tending slowly but surely to make the Eastern domain Polish.   To have warded off a danger which threatened, is often in politics a greater success than to achieve a momentary advantage.

If the attempt to extend Polish nationality had not been met by the Government with a determined effort to extend German nationality, things in Posen and West Prussia to-day would have been much the same as in Galicia. It is quite comprehensible that the Austrian monarchy, which is not a State based on a foundation of one nationality, has, for reasons of home and foreign policy, renounced all further attempts to Germanise the Crown land of Galicia since the 'seventies, and has responded in the most lavish manner to Polish wishes. Prussia is the support of the German Empire and of the national idea, is the German national State, κατ' ἐξοχήν, and cannot grant such concessions without being false to her past, her traditions, and her German mission.

Prussia must be ruled and administered from the national German standpoint. If we had allowed the Slavonic element in the East of the Prussian Kingdom to extend and flood the German element, as has happened in part of Cisleithania, instead of having a hard fight for German nationality in the Eastern

Marches to-day, we should have had a fight to maintain the unity of the Prussian State; we should not have had a Polish problem, we should have had a Polish danger.

THE POLICY IN THE EASTERN MARCHES A NATIONAL DUTY FOR GERMANS.

Our policy in the Eastern Marches is a national duty which the German nation owes to itself. A highly cultured and strong nation may not, without a struggle, give up national possessions, once they have been acquired; it must have such belief in the power of its national culture, and such faith in its own strength, that it feels itself capable of, and justified in, enriching them. Whether we hold fast to our possessions in the East or not, whether our policy in the Eastern Marches continues in its national course, what is to become of our Eastern Marches—these are not questions of party politics, but of general national importance; and not only the fate of the Germans in the East of Prussia, but the future of Prussia and of the Empire, nay, of the whole German nation, depend on whether these questions are answered in the affirmative or in the negative. In my opinion, as

I said in January, 1902, the problem of the Eastern Marches is not only one of our most important political problems, but, what is more, it is the problem on the solution and development of which the immediate future of our country depends.

CONCLUSION

CONCLUSION

THE German Empire, such as it emerged from the
baptism of fire of Königgrätz and Sedan, the belated fruit of the slow evolution of our nation, could
not come into existence until German intellect and
the Prussian monarchy joined forces. They were
bound to join forces if a united German State of lasting power was to be achieved. German history,
eventful as it is, discloses an abundance of great and
mighty deeds: the struggle of the German Emperors
for the heritage of the Cæsars, German arms victorious on the shores of the Great Belt and the Mediterranean, in Asia Minor, and in the heart of what is now
France; and after the intellectual refining process of
the Reformation, the greatest development of artistic
and scientific life that the world has known since the
days of Hellas and the Cinquecento. But the result,
as far as the State and politics are concerned, was the
dissolution of all forms of government in the nineteenth century, and the fact that German power was
outstripped by the younger States of Eastern and
Western Europe. In a thousand years of work,

from the point of view of culture, the highest had been accomplished, but politically, nothing had been achieved. The Western and Southern domains of Germany, greatly favoured by Nature, accomplished indestructible work in the sphere of German intellectual life, but could not raise sufficient strength for the sterner business of creating a State. We modern Germans do not share Treitschke's harsh opinion that the small German States were worthless. During the decades in which we have enjoyed union as an Empire, we have recovered a clear perception of the manifold blessings we owe to the small States. Side by side with the sins of German separatism we must place the encouragement and protection afforded to the intellectual life of Germany by the Princes and the cities. The Court of the Muses at Weimar achieved the highest in this respect, but it by no means stood alone.

The history of most of the non-Prussian States is connected with the name of some one or other of the men of Science and of Art who have helped to raise the magnificent edifice of our intellectual life. When Prussia woke to a consciousness of her duties with regard to the spiritual achievements of Germany, in those terrible but yet splendid years when, as Fred-

erick William III. so well expressed it, the Prussian
State must make good by its intellectual powers what
it had lost physically. German intellect had already
reached its zenith without the help of Prussia. German intellectual life, which the whole world has
learned to admire, and which even the first Napoleon
respected, is the work of the Southern and Western
German domains, achieved under the protection of
her Princes, small States, and free cities.

But the people who lived on the sandy soil of the
Marches, in the plains east of the Elbe and the Oder,
so scantly favoured by Nature, during the centuries
which witnessed the growth of German culture in
other parts of the country, prepared the future of
Germany as a State in battles and privations under
the rule of heroic and politic Kings.

German intellect was developed in the West and
the South, the German State in Prussia. The Princes
of the West were the patrons of German culture; the
Hohenzollern were the political teachers and task-
masters.

It took a long time before the importance of Prussia, in which even Goethe only loved her great King,
was recognised in Germany; before it was realised
that this rude and thoroughly prosaic State of soldiers

and officials, without many words but with deeds that were all the greater, was performing a task of enormous importance in the work of German civilisation: preparing the political culture of the German nation. Prussia became for Germany what Rome was for the ancient world. Leopold v. Ranke, intellectually the most versatile and at the same time the most Prussian of German historians, says, in his "History of the World," that it was the task of antiquity to permeate the Greek spirit with the Roman. Classical culture, in which the intellectual life of Western Europe is rooted, was preserved by the military and constitutional State of Rome, which gave to the ancient world its political shape. The Prussian State became the guardian of German intellectual life, by giving to the German people a united State and a position on a level with the great Empires of the world.

Through the foundation of the Empire we acquired national life as a State. In so doing our political development embarked on a new and a safe course. But it has not yet reached its goal. Our task, which has been begun but is by no means yet completed, must be the unity of our intellectual and political life, that is the fusion of the Prussian and the German spirit. Prussian State life and German intellectual

life must become reconciled in such a way that both
their growths become intertwined without weakening
each other.

Such a reconciliation has not yet been achieved.
The representative of German intellectual life is still
sometimes inclined to regard the Prussian State as a
hostile power, and the old Prussian at times to regard
the free and untrammelled development of German
intellect as a destructive force. And again and again
in Parliament and in the Press accusations are lev-
elled against Prussia in the name of freedom, and
against the undaunted German intellect in the name
of order.

My late friend, Adolph Wilbrandt, in a pleasing
play, has a scene between an official belonging to the
North German nobility and the daughter of a savant
of the middle classes. At first they repel each other
and quarrel. "I represent the Germany of Schiller,
Goethe and Lessing," says the woman, and the man
replies: "And I represent the Germany of Bismarck,
Blücher and Moltke." We often hear similar things
from the lips of clever and serious men. Our future
depends on whether, and to what extent, we succeed in
amalgamating German intellect with the Prussian
monarchy. Wilbrandt's play ends with the love and

marriage of the budding Minister of State and the charming enthusiast for Friedrich Schiller.

It is quite true that in many cases in non-Prussian Germany, owing to other political traditions, conceptions of State rule and freedom prevail that are fundamentally different from those that have sprung from the soil of Prussian traditions. This distinction is found, not only in party differences, but in the parties themselves. In the South of Germany there is a tendency to slacken the reins of political powers below, in Prussia a tendency to tighten them from above. In the former case a conception of political life more from the intellectual standpoint; in the latter more from the standpoint of the State. Each of them is the result of historical growth and is justified in its peculiarity. The Prussian does wrong if he refuses to see anything but destructive democracy in the political life of South Germany: the South German is equally wrong if he exclaims in horror at the antiquated politics of Prussian State life.

Progress in political life is a very fluid idea, and in what direction of political development true progress will lie is more than all the wise men of the world can tell. Each State, each nation tries to advance in its own way and to perfect its political institutions.

We Germans, who for historical reasons have not a uniform but a manifold political life, are the last nation in the world that can afford to indulge in abstract political principles, either such as are derived only from Prussian or such as are derived only from South German traditions, and to fit all politics to these principles. It is our task to conduct political development in Prussia, the individual States and the Empire in such a way that in each member of the Empire those forces are preserved which tend to make it most valuable to the Fatherland in general. Harmony of German life in all its parts must be attained, not so much by making all institutions in the north, south, east and west uniform, as in smoothing the differences that still exist.

Bismarck's foundation of the Empire was not least masterly in that it created a firm bond of union, while at the same time it did not destroy the peculiarities and the independence of the individual States; and also in that it not only nominally, but actually, made Prussia the leading State by preserving the monarchical principle in the new Empire.

The union of Germany that the patriotic Democrats of the 'forties conceived in the nineteenth century was to do away with the independence of the

Federal States, more or less, and to vest the unifying power in the paramount influence of an Imperial Parliament. Apart from the fact that the German Princes would never have consented to such a union, it was a mistake in a thoroughly monarchical country like Germany to expect unifying power from parliamentary life which had no existence, and therefore had never been tested.

That in a common representative assembly of the German people the forces tend rather to separate than to unite in the idea of the Empire and in great national tasks, has been amply proved by the struggles between the Imperial Government and the parties in the Reichstag during the years which have passed since the founding of the Empire. Bismarck, the Prussian, realised better than anyone else that in Germany strong government could only be based and maintained on the monarchical principle. The work of union could only be permanent if the monarchy was not a purely ornamental part of the fabric of the Empire, but was made to be the actual support of the union. And if the creative power of Prussian monarchy, well tested in the course of centuries, was to be enlisted in the interests of the new Empire, then the King of Prussia must, as German Emperor, be more than the bearer of shadowy dignities; he must rule and guide—and for this purpose must actually possess monarchical rights such as have been laid down and transcribed in the Constitution of the Empire.

Germany would never, or at best very slowly and imperfectly, have achieved union as a State by following the paths of democracy along which other nations have reached the goal of national development. As a monarchy, with the federal Princes represented in the Federal Council, and the King of Prussia at the head, we have become a united German Empire. Had we been entrusted entirely to the care of quarrelling parties in Parliament, the idea of the Empire would never have gained so much ground, would never have been able to win the heart of Germans to such an extent as is actually the case, since the unity of the Empire was placed under the protection of the monarchy. At the beginning of the 'sixties, in the nineteenth century, Crispi, later President of the Ministry in Italy, a country whose fate has a resemblance to Germany's, wrote to Mazzini that he had been converted from the Republic to the Monarchy, because the latter would unite Italy, whereas the former would disintegrate her: the same applies to us. And it is particularly true in our case because the German Empire, situated in the middle of Europe, and insufficiently protected by nature on its frontiers, is and must remain a military State. And in history strong military States have always required monarchical guidance.

A strong monarchy at the head of affairs by no means precludes a lively interest on the part of the people in the political life of the Empire and the individual States. On the contrary, the more keen and intelligent the interest that all classes of the nation take in the development of political matters, the closer will grow the ties between the people and the monarchy, which as leader and guide stands at the head of national life. Political life in a modern monarchy, as created by our Constitution, entails co-operation between the Crown and the people. It is an old mistake to want to gauge the concern of the nation in political affairs solely by the rights granted to the representatives of the people. A Parliament may possess very extensive rights and yet the nation may take very little interest in politics. Thus in France formerly, Parliament was sometimes all-powerful, whereas the people were indifferent. The relatively large measure of constitutional rights which the Reichstag and the Diets in Germany enjoy might be accompanied by far keener political interest and far deeper political understanding on the part of the nation, than has hitherto been the case. The so-called "politification of the people" is a matter of political education, not a question of parliamentary power.

The statement uttered from time to time, that my idea was to change the distribution of power between the Crown and the Parliament in favour of the latter, that is, to introduce parliamentary government in the West European sense of the words, belongs to the thickly populated realm of political fables. In my eyes the dividing line between the rights of the Crown and of Parliament was immutably fixed. In foreign as well as in home politics I considered it my noblest task, to the best of my understanding and ability, to strengthen, support and protect the Crown, not only on account of deep loyalty and personal affection for the wearer, but also because I see in the Crown the corner stone of Prussia and the keystone of the Empire.

What we Germans need cannot be attained by alterations in the sphere of constitutional law. The parties which would acquire greater rights, to a large extent still lack political judgment, political training and consciousness of the aims of the State. In Germany a large number of educated people, who ought to play a leading part in party life, still adopt an attitude of indifference, if not of dislike towards politics. Very clever men often assert with a certain pride that they understand nothing and wish to know nothing of politics. The ignorance which prevails in regard to the most elementary matters of government is often astounding.

Those times are past when it was of no concern to the welfare of the State whether the nation did or did not understand the laws under which it lived. Legislation no longer lies exclusively in the hands of specially trained and experienced officials; Parliament co-operates in the task. But the work of the factions is even now carried out much as the work of the officials alone used to be formerly: to the accompaniment of a complete lack of understanding and judgment on the part of large sections of the community. In connection with economic questions, it is true groups that are interested in agriculture, commerce and industry display a certain amount of activity, as do associations formed for special purposes when matters connected with these special purposes are in question; for the most part, however, the dictum of the Members of Parliament is accepted quite passively by the

limited understanding of the common herd. But, as
soon as the tangible effects are felt, bitter criticism is
heard, which, however, is limited to the individual case
and does not result in any stimulation of political understanding.

What we Germans lack is active interest in the
course of political affairs, interest that is not only
aroused at elections which take place at considerable
intervals, but that is concerned with all the great and
small questions of political life. It is the duty of the
educated classes to take this political education in
hand—the duty of the intellectual leaders, whom the
Germans follow more readily than does any other
nation. The indolent indifference towards political
life of men who are æsthetically and intellectually
sensitive, though in earlier times it was harmless, is
now out of place. The present, which is full of grave
and great political tasks, and which has, by means of
Parliaments, given the people a share in State affairs,
demands a political generation. It is not the duty of
the Government in the present time to concede new
rights to Parliament, but to rouse the political interest
of all classes of the nation by means of a vigorous and
determined national policy, great in its aims and energetic in the means it employs. The criticism to

which every policy that is not colourless must give rise does no harm, so long as positive interest is aroused. The worst thing in political life is torpor, a general and stifling calm.

Rest is only permissible to him who has no more duties to fulfil. No nation can assert that of itself, least of all the Germans who so recently embarked on a new course towards new goals. The number of problems we have solved since 1870 is small compared with the number that still await solution. We may only rejoice in what has been accomplished if the sight of what we can do gives us faith in our power to achieve more and greater things. Goethe depicted the German nation as a man, not in Wagner, who is filled with satisfaction by the contemplation of the splendid things he has ultimately accomplished, but in Faust, who, with high self-confidence, is always at pains to achieve greater things, and, as the ultimate conclusion of wisdom, gives utterance to the truth that: "He alone deserves liberty and life who must conquer them daily anew."

THE END